FELT TOY MAKING

FELT TOY MAKING
ADVANCED TECHNIQUES

BY

AMY VAN GILDER

Amy Van Gilder

PHOTOGRAPHY BY

RACKET SHREVE

DRAKE PUBLISHERS INC NEW YORK

PUBLISHED IN 1974 BY
DRAKE PUBLISHERS INC.
381 PARK AVENUE SOUTH
NEW YORK, NEW YORK 10016

LIBRARY OF CONGRESS CATALOGING IN PUBLICATION DATA
VAN GILDER, AMY.
   FELT TOYMAKING : ADVANCED TECHNIQUES.

   1. SOFT TOY MAKING. 2. FELT WORK. I. TITLE.
TT174.3.V36   745.59'22   74-6077
ISBN 0-87749-672-2

PRINTED IN BRAZIL.

TABLE OF CONTENTS

GENERAL INSTRUCTIONS
(and SIMPLIFICATION HINTS)

1. EVERYTHING IS STITCHED BY MACHINE UNLESS SPECIFICALLY STATED OTHERWISE.

2. SEAM ALLOWANCE IS A CONSISTENT 3/16".

3. ALL SEAMS, EXCEPT WHERE SPECIFICALLY STATED TO THE CONTRARY, ARE STITCHED SO THAT THE SEAM ALLOWANCE IS ON THE OUTSIDE OF THE PROJECT. THIS IS ONE OF THE JOYS OF FELT — NO RAVELING AND MINIMAL TURNING.

4. ALWAYS TACK EVERYTHING AT THE START OF STITCHING AND THE END (ie. MAKE MACHINE GO BACK AND FORTH AT BEGINNING AND END OF <u>EVERY</u> LINE OF STITCHING.) OTHERWISE YOUR PROJECTS WILL FALL APART.

5. IN CASES WHERE WIRE IS USED, FOLLOW THE DIRECTIONS EXACTLY. IF WIRE IS HANDLED CORRECTLY, NO ONE WILL BE POKED OR SCRATCHED.

6. BLACK THREAD IS USED ON MOST PROJECTS THROUGHOUT THIS BOOK. THE DEADLINE WOULDN'T HAVE BEEN MET OTHERWISE. CHOICE OF THREAD COLOR IS UP TO YOU.

7. BASICALLY, YOU WILL NEED A SEWING MACHINE, ZIPPER FOOT, PINS, NEEDLES, TRACING PAPER, THREAD, SCISSORS, PENCILS, A STUFFING POKER, 50% WOOL/50% RAYON FELT, SPRAY ADHESIVE AND PATIENCE TO COMPLETE THESE PROJECTS.

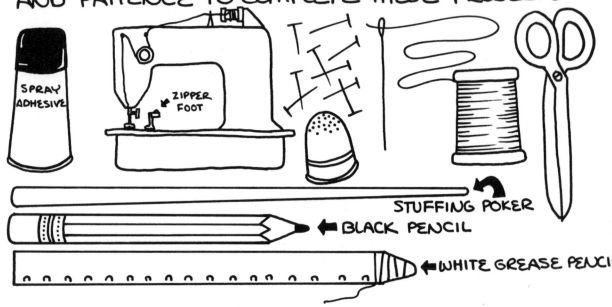

SPRAY ADHESIVE

ZIPPER FOOT

STUFFING POKER

← BLACK PENCIL

←WHITE GREASE PENCIL

8. YOU WILL HAVE TO TRACE THE PATTERNS OUT OF THIS BOOK. TRACING PAPER PATTERNS ARE SATISFACTORY TO PIN AND CUT AROUND. HOWEVER, IF YOU PREFER DRAWING PATTERN OUTLINES ON THE FELT, SPRAY THE BACK OF THE TRACING PAPER PATTERN WITH ADHESIVE, STICK IT TO A PIECE OF CARDBOARD AND CUT AROUND THE OUTLINE. CRACKER OR CEREAL BOXES ARE A GOOD WEIGHT CARDBOARD FOR PATTERNS.

9. TO KEEP PATTERN PIECES FOR EACH PROJECT TO- GETHER, PUNCH HOLES IN ALL THE PIECES AND SAFETY PIN THEM TOGETHER.

10. IN FIVE INSTANCES IN THIS BOOK, THE PATTERN PIECE, AS A WHOLE, DOES NOT FIT ONTO ONE PAGE. THESE SITUATIONS ARE CLEARLY INDICATED. WHEN TRACING THESE PATTERNS OFF THE PAGE, COMBINE THE TWO PARTS TO MAKE THE COMPLETE PATTERN.

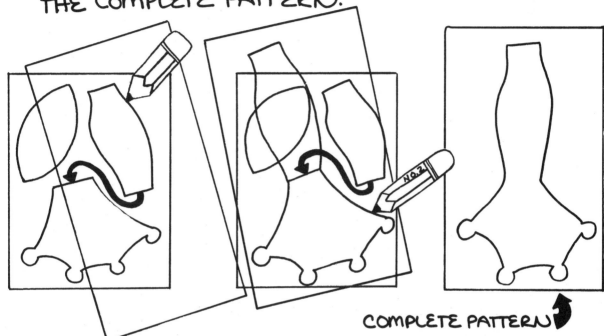

COMPLETE PATTERN

11. SOME PATTERN PIECES SAY "PLACE ON FOLD". THIS WAS DONE TO FIT MORE PIECES ON THE PAGE. IF YOU PLACE THE PATTERN PIECE ON A FOLD OF <u>TRACING PAPER</u>, IT WILL SIMPLIFY THE CUTTING. INSTEAD OF FOLDING THE FELT, YOU WILL BE WORKING WITH A FULL PATTERN.

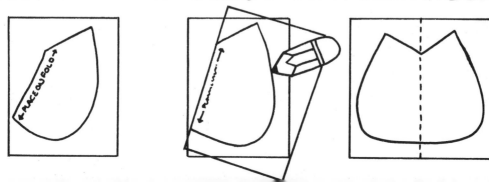

PEOPLE PUPPET

YOU WILL NEED:
10"x15" FELT FOR BASIC PUPPET
SCRAPS OF PINK, WHITE, AND BLACK FELT

INSTRUCTIONS FOR BASIC PUPPET :

1. PLACE TONGUE (#**1**) BETWEEN INSIDES OF MOUTH (#**2**). STITCH.

2. STITCH EYES TO FACE (#**3**).

3. INVENT AND ATTACH NOSE.

4. STITCH PIECE #**4** TO #**5**. PLACE WRONG SIDE OF #**4** AGAINST RIGHT SIDE OF #**5**.

5. STITCH HALF OF MOUTH TO #**4**.

6. STITCH OTHER HALF OF MOUTH TO #**3**.

7. INVENT AND ATTACH HAIR.

8. PIN AND STITCH FRONT TO BACK (#**6**). STITCH FROM **A** TO **B**. LIFT THREAD. STITCH FROM **B** TO **C**. LIFT THREAD. STITCH FROM **C** TO **D**.

<u>PATTERN PIECES INCLUDED</u> AS **ALTERNATIVES**

<u>EARS</u> – SINGLE LAYER OR STUFFED

<u>HAIR</u> - STITCH #**9** OR #**10** TO BODY BACK

<u>EYELIDS</u> - <u>TEETH</u>

<u>HANDS</u> - STUFFED AND STITCHED INTO SIDES OR PATTERN PIECES #**5a** AND #**6a** FOR EMPTY ARMS FOR FINGERS.

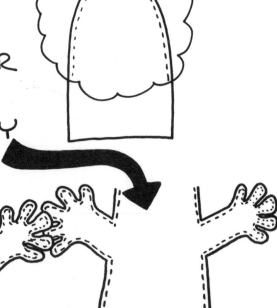

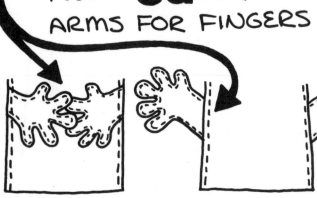

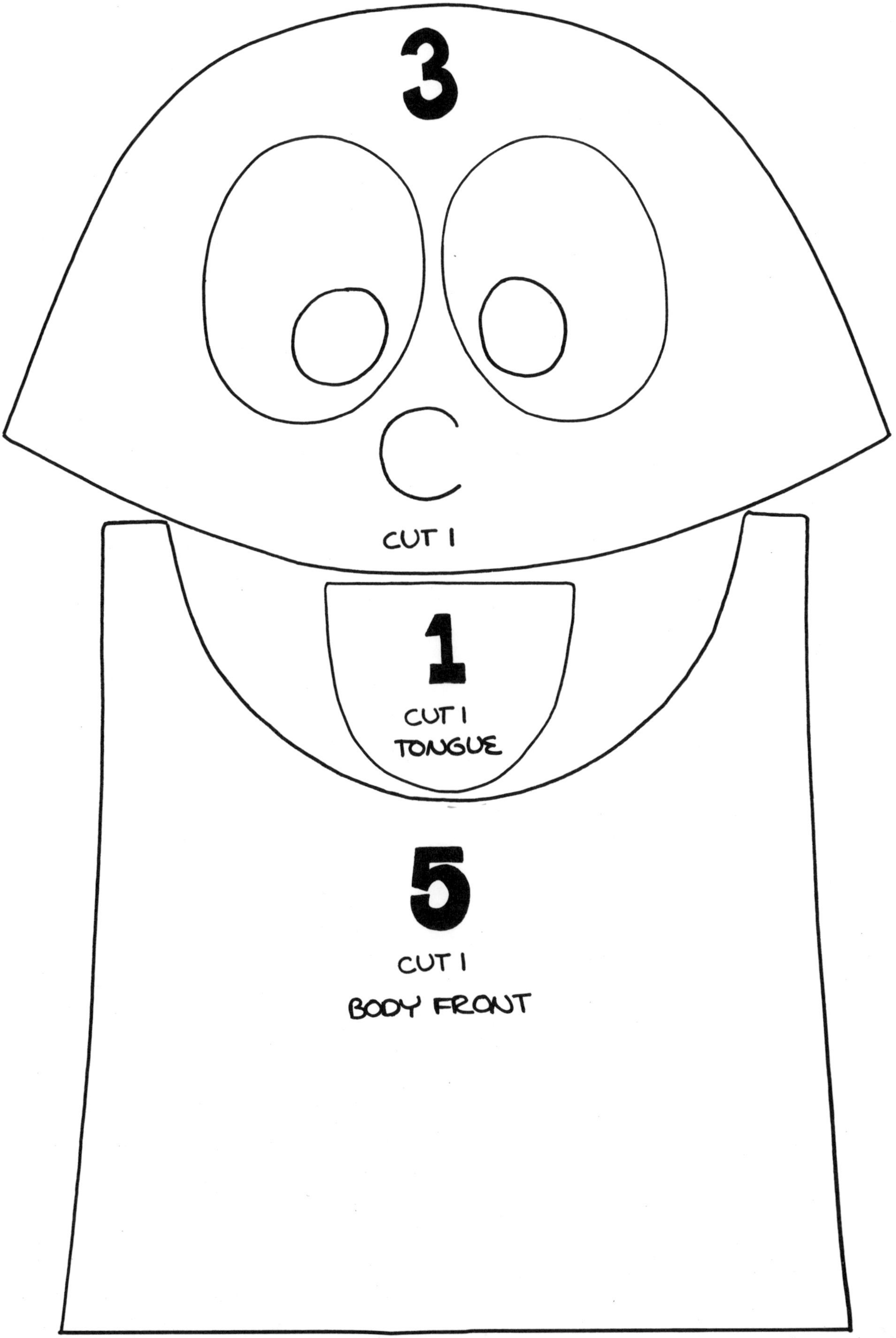

3

CUT 1

1

CUT 1
TONGUE

5

CUT 1

BODY FRONT

6

CUT 1

BODY BACK

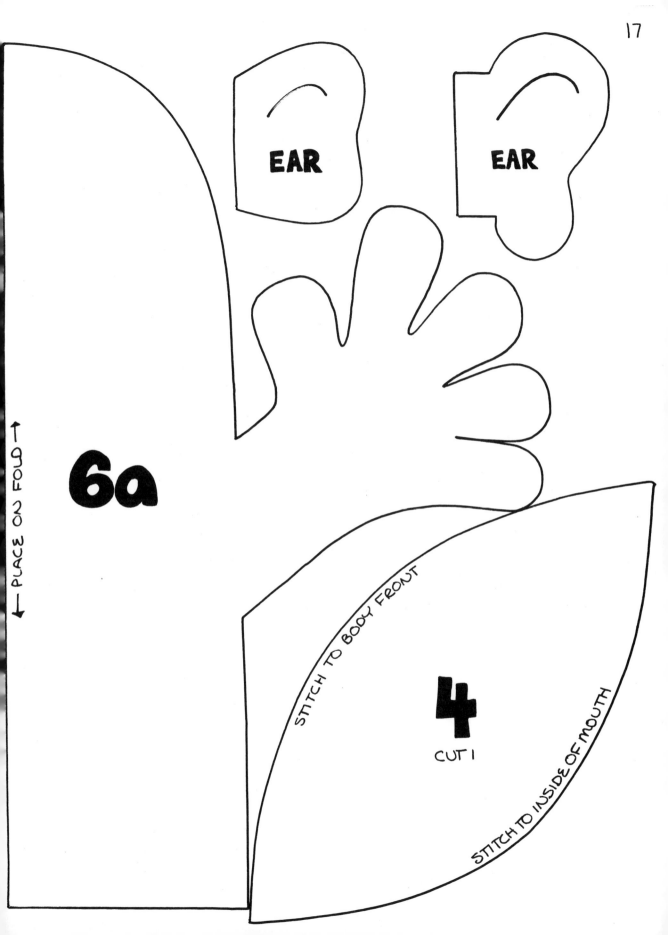

EAR

EAR

6a

← PLACE ON FOLD →

STITCH TO BODY FRONT

4

CUT 1

STITCH TO INSIDE OF MOUTH

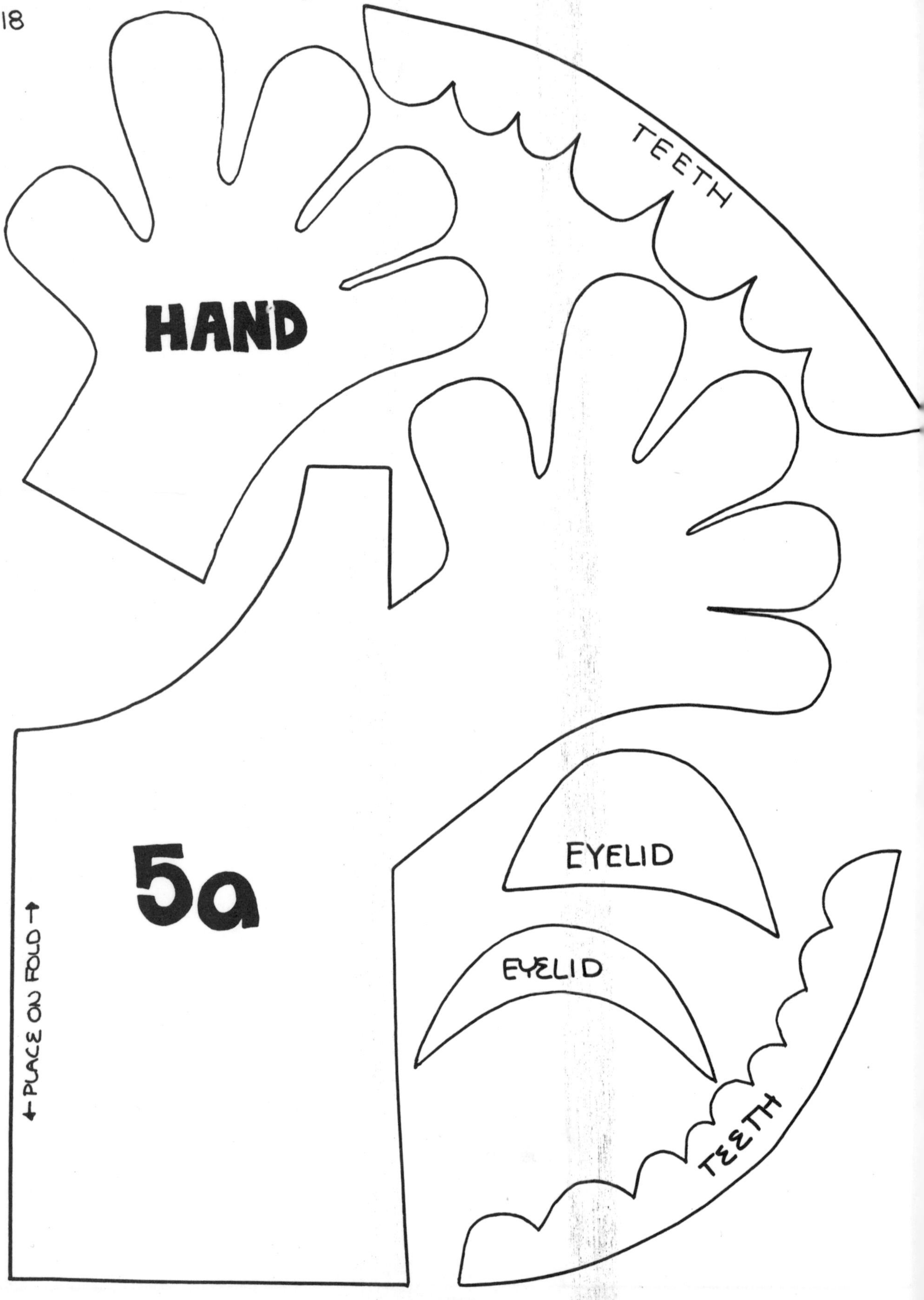

18

HAND

TEETH

5a

← PLACE ON FOLD →

EYELID

EYELID

TEETH

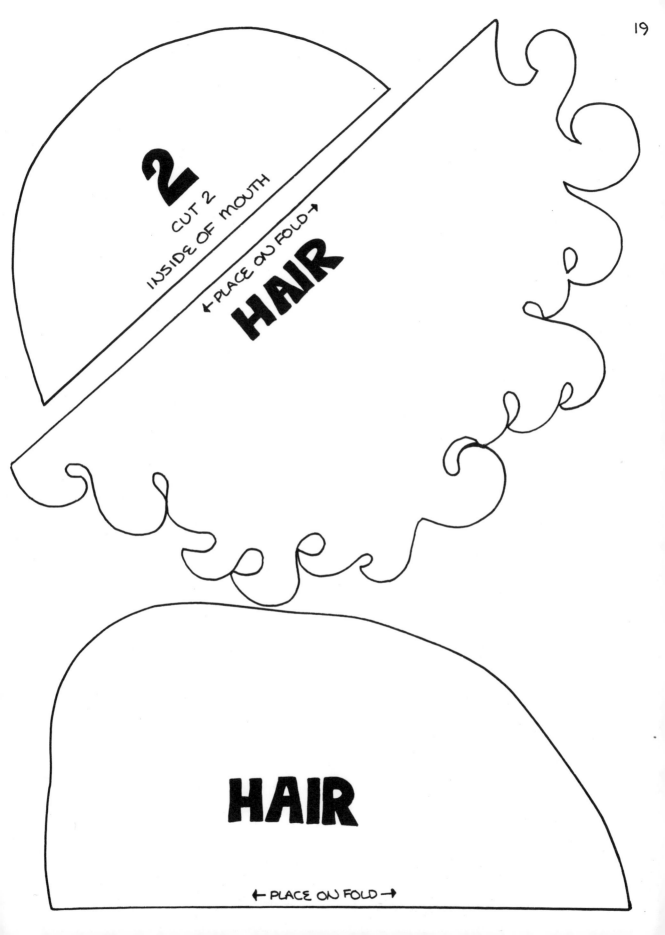

ROSE PUPPET

YOU WILL NEED:

8" x 36" LIGHT PETAL COLOR
6" x 18" DARK PETAL COLOR
8" x 16" DARK GREEN
7" x 12" LIGHT GREEN
BLACK, WHITE AND ORANGE
   OR YELLOW FELT SCRAPS
7½" 20 GAUGE WIRE

1. STITCH FOUR INNER PETALS (#**1**) TO FOUR OUTER PETALS (#**2**).

2. BEND OVER ENDS OF WIRE ¼".

3. PLACE INNER LEAF (#**8**) OVER LEAF CLUSTER (#**9**). STITCH FROM STEM TO END OF LEAF. TAKE THREE STITCHES ACROSS.

PRESS WIRE AGAINST LINE OF STITCHING. STITCH DOWN OTHER SIDE.

4. ATTACH OTHER LEAVES (#**10**, #**11**) WITH STRAIGHT LINES OF STITCHING.

22

5. STITCH STAMENS (#**3**) BETWEEN INSIDES OF MOUTH (#**4**).

 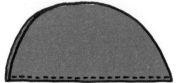

6. STITCH EYES TO FACE (#**5**).

7. PIN AND STITCH #**5** TO ONE HALF OF INSIDE OF MOUTH. (PIN IN CENTER THEN PIN OUT TO EACH SIDE.)

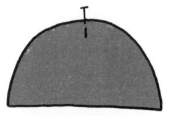 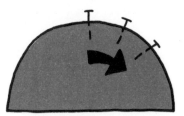

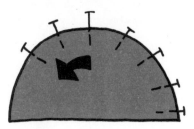 

8. PIN TWO PETALS TO FRONT STEM (#**6**).

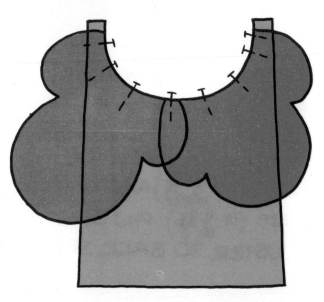

9. PIN RIGHT SIDE OF #**7** OVER THE PETALS AND #**6**. STITCH.

10. STITCH OTHER HALF OF INSIDE OF MOUTH TO #**7**.

11. PIN BIGGEST PETAL (#**12**) AND INSIDE OF BIGGEST PETAL (#**13**) AGAINST BACK STEM (#**14**). PIN LEAF CLUSTER TO BACK STEM.

DON'T PANIC JUST KEEP PINNING

11. PIN FRONT OF STEM (WITH PETALS AND FACE) TO BACK (WITH PETALS AND LEAF CLUSTER).

12. PIN THIRD PETAL OF #**1**, #**2** COMBINATION OVER EVERYTHING ELSE.

25

13. PIN REMAINING PETAL OVER LEAF AND THIRD PETAL.

14. STITCH ALL THE WAY AROUND THE ROSE, FROM **A** TO **B**. DON'T STITCH OVER PETALS.

A   B

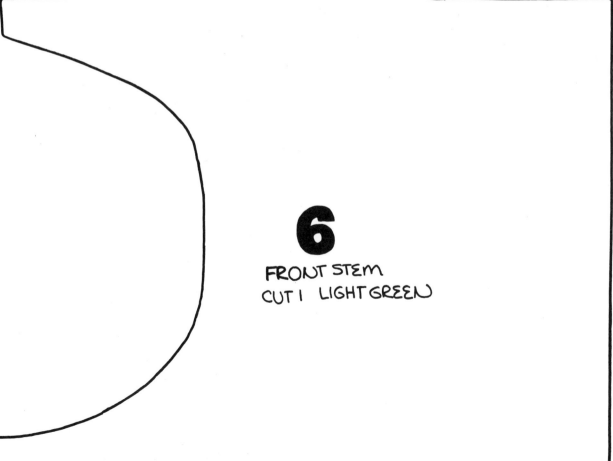

6

FRONT STEM
CUT I LIGHT GREEN

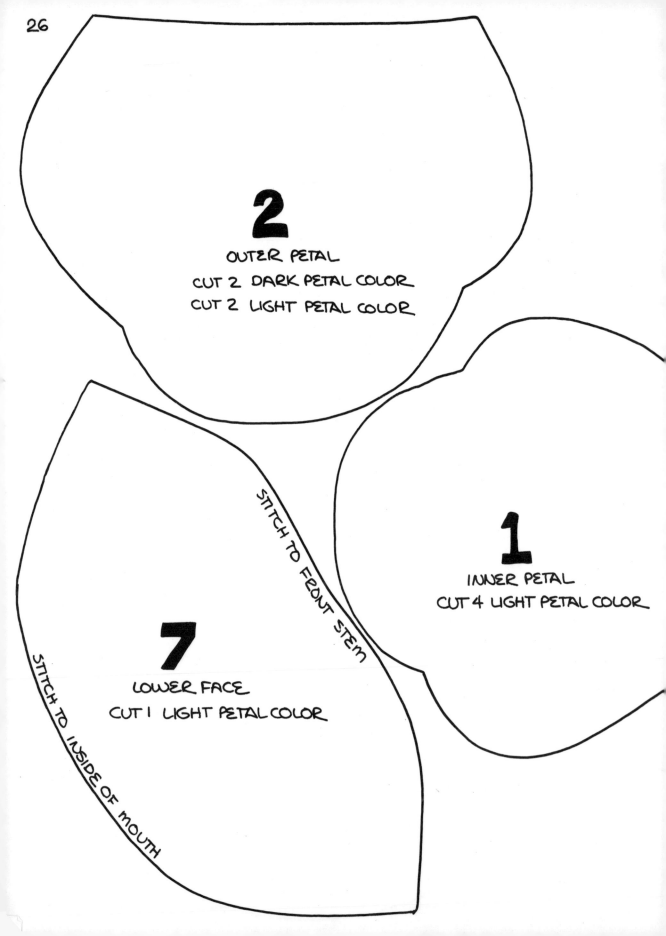

2

OUTER PETAL

CUT 2 DARK PETAL COLOR

CUT 2 LIGHT PETAL COLOR

1

INNER PETAL

CUT 4 LIGHT PETAL COLOR

7

LOWER FACE

CUT 1 LIGHT PETAL COLOR

STITCH TO FRONT STEM

STITCH TO INSIDE OF MOUTH

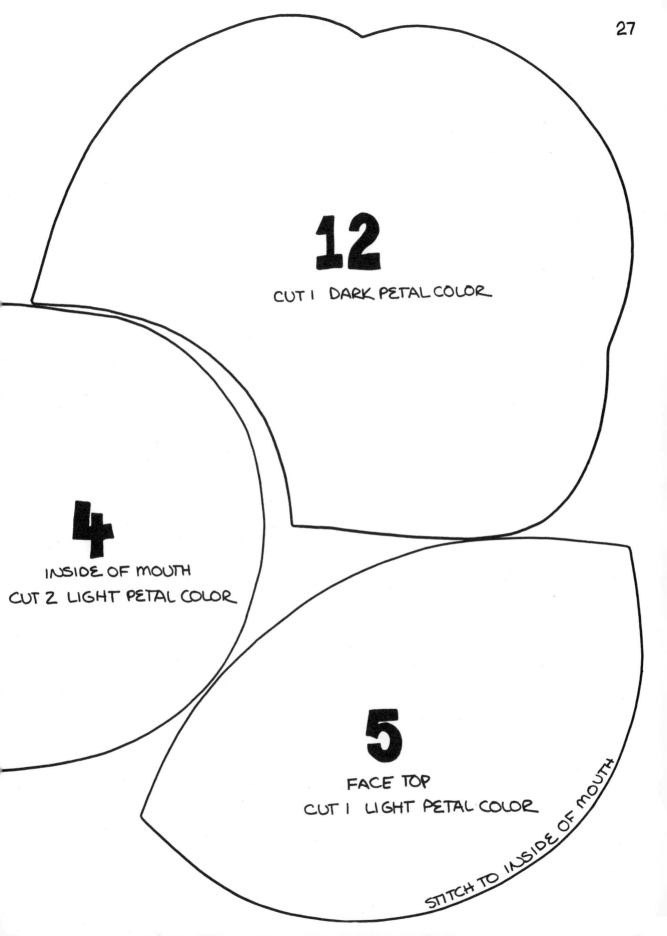

12

CUT 1   DARK PETAL COLOR

4

INSIDE OF MOUTH

CUT 2 LIGHT PETAL COLOR

5

FACE TOP

CUT 1 LIGHT PETAL COLOR

STITCH TO INSIDE OF MOUTH

28

3

STAMEN CUT 5

CUT 2
EYE
BLACK

EYE
CUT 2
WHITE

14

BACK STEM

CUT 1 DARK GREEN

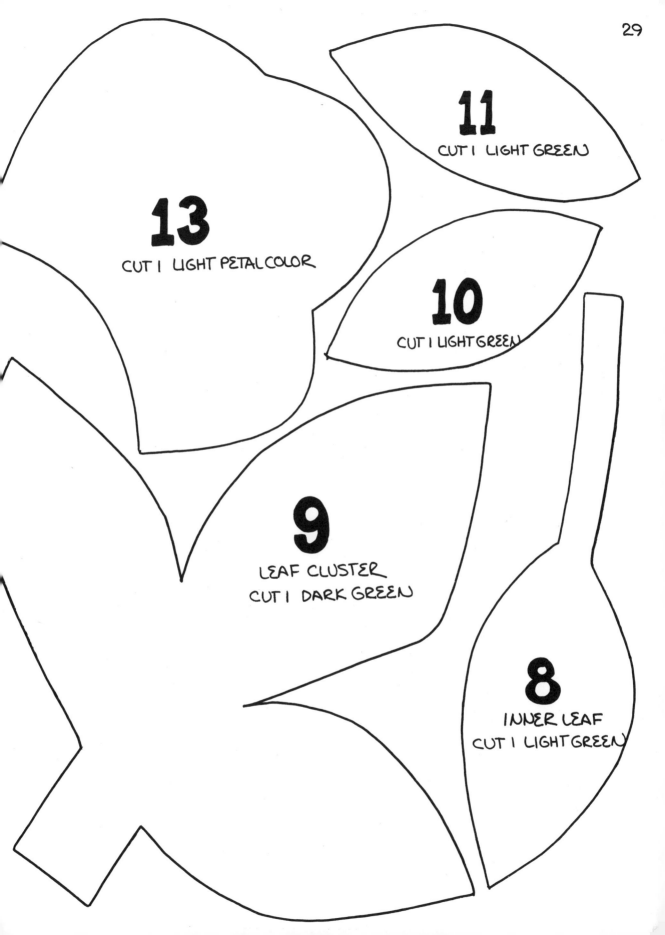

11
CUT 1 LIGHT GREEN

13
CUT 1 LIGHT PETAL COLOR

10
CUT 1 LIGHT GREEN

9
LEAF CLUSTER
CUT 1 DARK GREEN

8
INNER LEAF
CUT 1 LIGHT GREEN

MONARCH BUTTERFLY PUPPET

YOU WILL NEED:
12"x 32" BLACK FELT
8"x10" ORANGE FELT
SCRAPS OF WHITE, PINK, YELLOW FELT
TWO 12" PIPE CLEANERS
(AVAILABLE WITH PARTY SUPPLIES)
17" OF 20 GAUGE WIRE

1. STITCH **A, B, C, M, N, O, P, Q, R** AND **S** TO FRONTS OF WINGS (#**7**, #**8**).

2. ATTACH EYES TO FACE (#**1**) BY MACHINE STITCHING AROUND BLACK DOTS.

3. STITCH BOTTOM OF FACE (#**2**) TO ONE INSIDE OF MOUTH (#**3**).

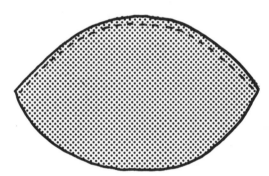

4. BEND OVER ONE PIPE CLEANER ¼" AT BOTH ENDS. CURL A PROBOSCIS.

5. PIN OTHER INSIDE OF MOUTH TO FACE. INSERT PROBOSCIS 1" AT CENTER OF MOUTH. STITCH. BE CAREFUL NOT TO BREAK YOUR SEWING MACHINE NEEDLE ON THE WIRE. AFTER PROBOSCIS IS STITCHED INTO SEAM, MACHINE TACK IT ¾" IN FROM SEAM.

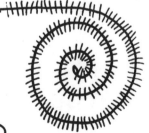

6. STITCH INSIDES OF MOUTH TOGETHER .

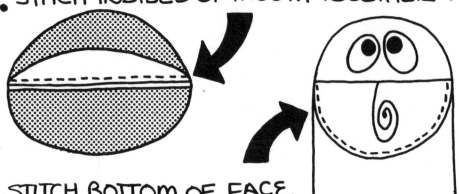

7. STITCH BOTTOM OF FACE (#**2**) TO BODY FRONT (#**4**). (PLACE WRONG SIDE OF #**2** AGAINST RIGHT SIDE OF #**4**.)

8. PIN WINGS TO BODY BACK (#**5**).

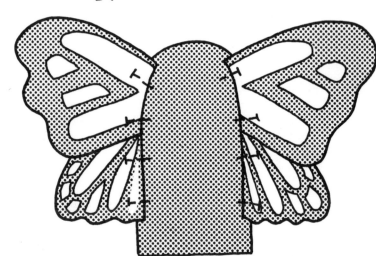

9. CUT SECOND PIPE CLEANER IN HALF. BEND OVER ¼" AT ONE END OF EACH. MAKE CIRCLES ½" IN DIAMETER AT OTHER ENDS. TWIST WIRE WITH PLIERS SO THERE ARE NO SHARP ENDS.

10. PIN FRONT TO BACK. PIN ANTENNAE BETWEEN FRONT AND BACK OF FACE AT ARROWS (INDICATED ON PATTERN PIECE #**1**).

11. STITCH FRONT AND BACK TOGETHER. STITCH FROM **A** TO **B**. LIFT THREAD. STITCH FROM **B** TO **C**. LIFT THREAD. STITCH FROM **C** TO **D**.

12. PIN #**6** TO BACK OF WINGS AND HEAD.

13. BEND ¼" OVER ON BOTH ENDS OF 17" WIRE.

SHAPE WIRE TO OUTLINE OF HEAD AND WINGS. FIT WIRE IN POCKET. USING A ZIPPER FOOT, STITCH THE WIRE INTO THE POCKET (ON THE RIGHT SIDE OF THE BUTTERFLY SO YOU DON'T SEW ACROSS THE EYEBALLS). TRIM POCKET.

14. CUT OUT YELLOW AND WHITE PIECES AS IN PHOTOGRAPH. HAND STITCH YELLOW AND WHITE PIECES TO WINGS.

1

CUT 1 BLACK

4

BODY FRONT
CUT 1 BLACK

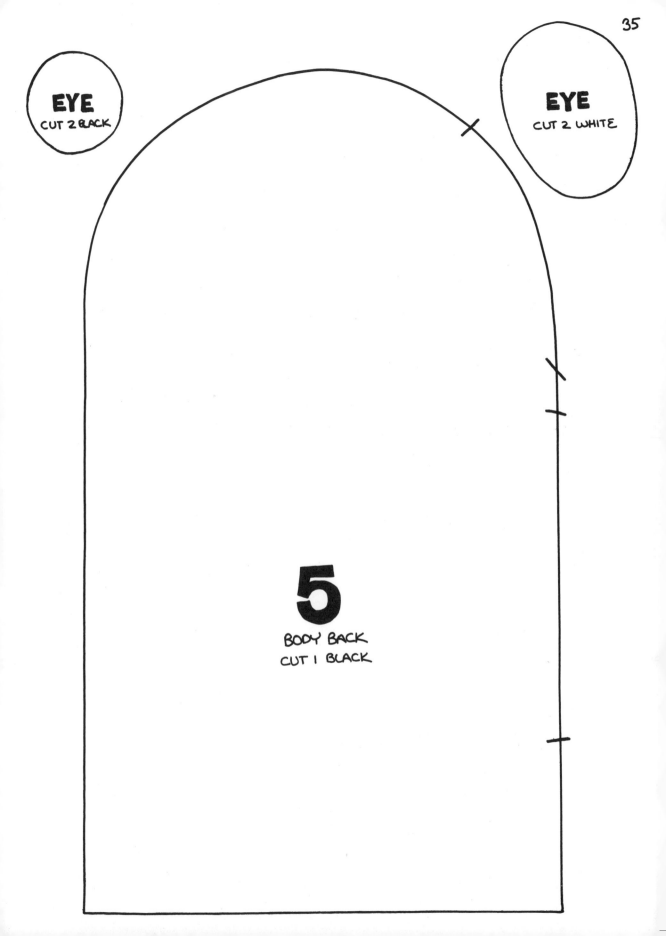

EYE
CUT 2 BLACK

EYE
CUT 2 WHITE

5
BODY BACK
CUT 1 BLACK

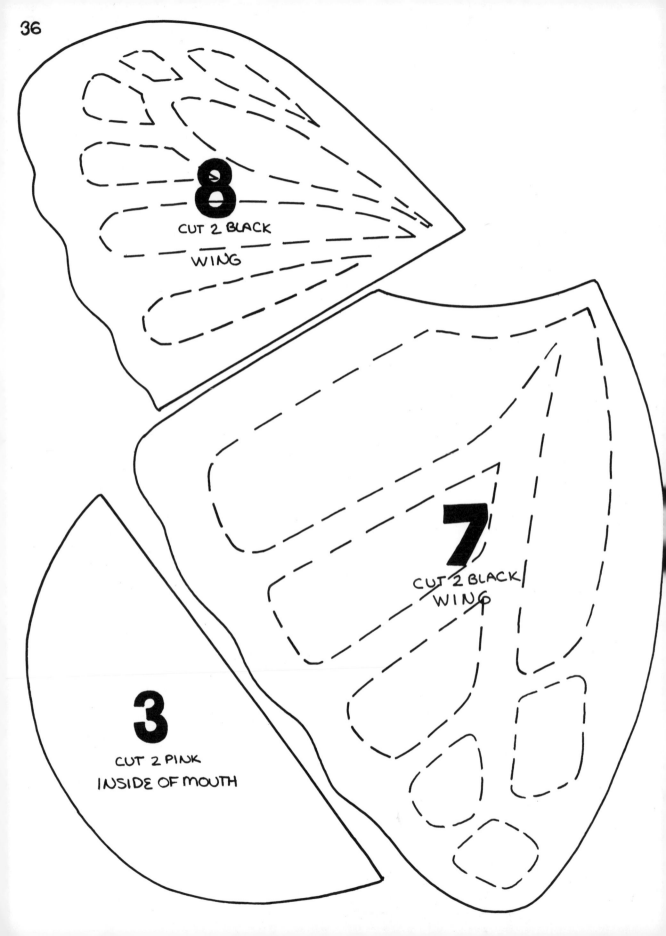

36

8
CUT 2 BLACK
WING

7
CUT 2 BLACK
WING

3
CUT 2 PINK
INSIDE OF MOUTH

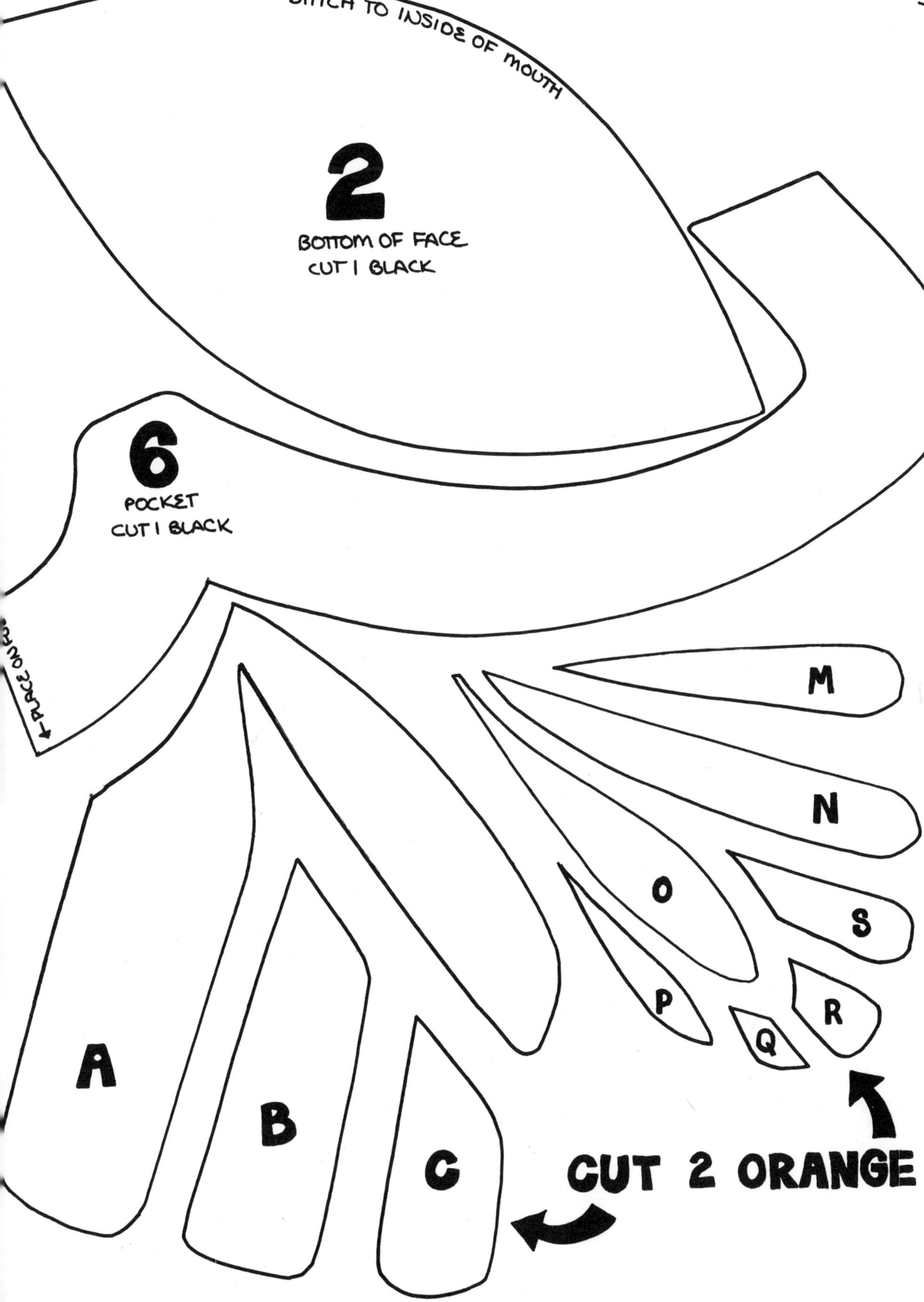

STITCH TO INSIDE OF MOUTH

2

BOTTOM OF FACE
CUT 1 BLACK

6

POCKET
CUT 1 BLACK

← PLACE ON FOLD

M

N

O

S

P

Q

R

A

B

C

CUT 2 ORANGE

BACHELOR'S BUTTON PUPPET

YOU WILL NEED:
10" x 19" BLUE FELT
6" x 9" LIGHT YELLOW FELT
12" x 13" GREEN FELT
PINK, BLACK, DARK YELLOW,
WHITE FELT SCRAPS
18" WIRE - 20 GAUGE
10" x 19" LIGHT WEIGHT
REGULAR INTERFACING

1. PIN PINWHEEL OF INTERFACING BETWEEN BLUE FELT PIECES #**1**.

2. STITCH FROM PETAL CORNER TO CORNER. DO NOT STITCH ACROSS ENDS.

3. SNIP ENDS IN BACHELOR BUTTONISH POINTS.

4. STITCH TONGUE (#**2**) BETWEEN INSIDES OF MOUTH (#**3**).

40

5. STITCH BOTTOM FACE (#**4**) TO ONE HALF OF INSIDE OF MOUTH.

6. STITCH TOP FACE (#**5**) TO OTHER HALF OF INSIDE OF MOUTH.

7. PLACE FACE ON BLUE PETALS AND PIN.

8. SPACE NINE STAMENS (#**6**) AROUND THE FACE. PIN AND STITCH.

9. FLIP THE FLOWER OVER AND CUT A HOLE ¼" FROM THE CIRCLE OF STITCHING.

10. PLACE FLOWER OVER BODY FRONT (#**7**). STITCH <u>OVER</u> LINE OF STITCHING AROUND FACE.

ENDS OF WIRE

11. FLIP FLOWER OVER AGAIN. CUT A HOLE IN GREEN FELT ¼" FROM STITCHING LINE.

(QUITE A REMARKABLE LOOKING THING FROM THE INSIDE OUT ISN'T IT.)

12. STITCH TOGETHER THE TWO HALVES OF #**8** WITH A LINE OF STITCHING JUST OFF CENTER.

13. FOLD THE 18" PIECE OF WIRE IN HALF. PLACE IT BETWEEN THE LEAF HALVES. SQUEEZE IT CLOSE TO THE EXISTING STITCHING LINE. TACK ACROSS TOP. STITCH DOWN OTHER SIDE.

14. PIN LEAF TO BODY BACK (#**7**). PIN BODY FRONT TO BODY BACK. STITCH AROUND BODY FROM **A** TO **B**. BE CAREFUL OF THE WIRE AND AVOID SEWING ACROSS PETALS.

15. ATTACH EYES.

A   **B**

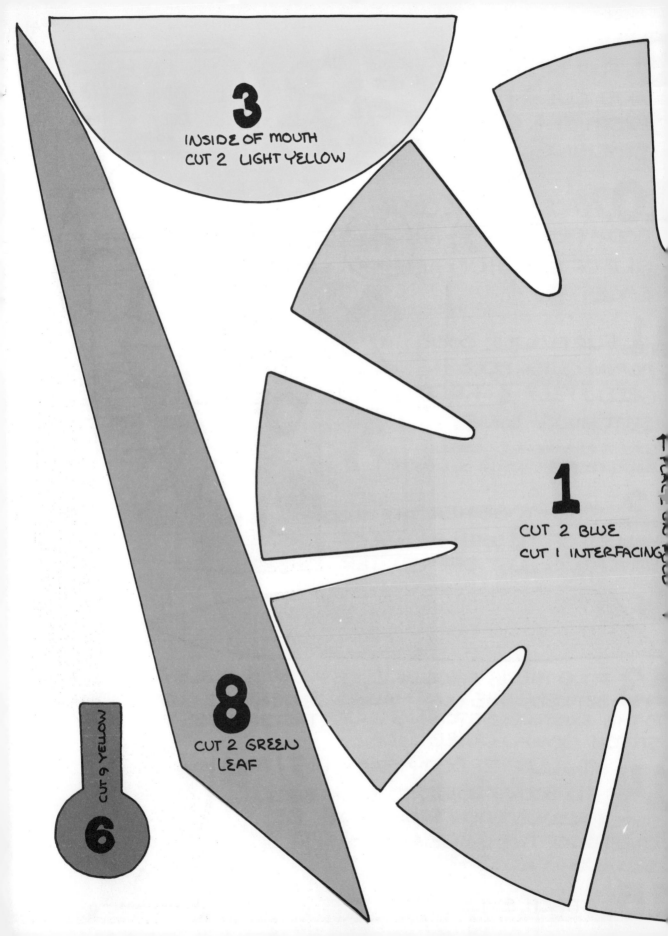

3

INSIDE OF MOUTH

CUT 2 LIGHT YELLOW

1

CUT 2 BLUE

CUT 1 INTERFACING

8

CUT 2 GREEN

LEAF

6

CUT 9 YELLOW

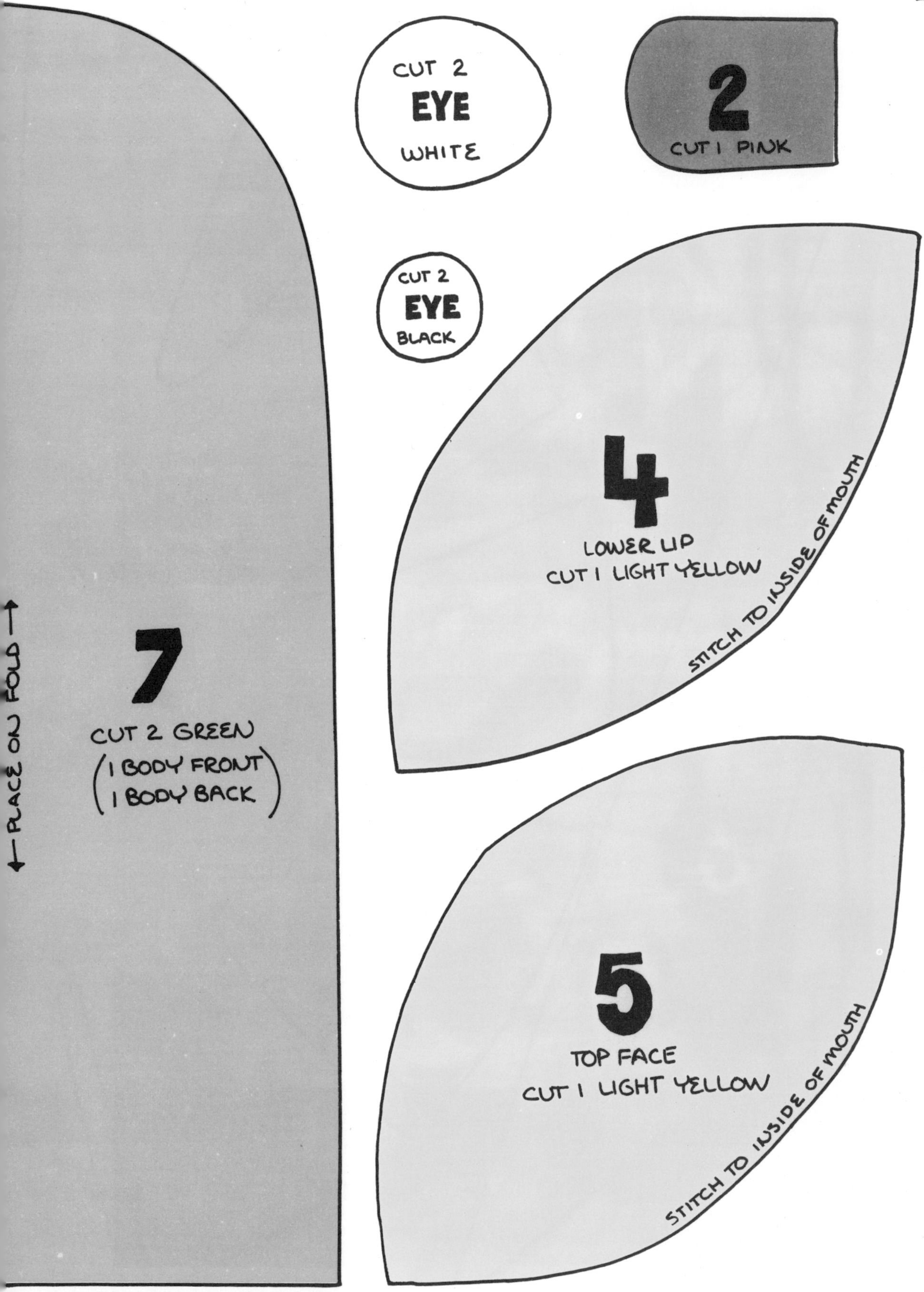

CUT 2
EYE
WHITE

2
CUT 1 PINK

CUT 2
EYE
BLACK

4
LOWER LIP
CUT 1 LIGHT YELLOW

STITCH TO INSIDE OF MOUTH

7
CUT 2 GREEN
(1 BODY FRONT)
(1 BODY BACK)

← PLACE ON FOLD →

5
TOP FACE
CUT 1 LIGHT YELLOW

STITCH TO INSIDE OF MOUTH

SOCK PUPPETS

FLOWER A

YOU WILL NEED:
POLYESTER FIBER FILL
ONE 100% STRETCH NYLON
   CHILD'S KNEE SOCK SIZE 6-7
FELT

1. STITCH TOGETHER RIGHT SIDES OF PATTERN PIECES #**1** ALONG CENTER FRONTS.

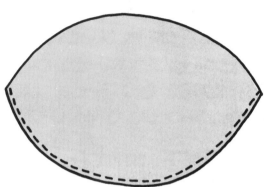

2. TURN RIGHT SIDE OUT. STITCH ON DOTS BY HAND. IF YOU HAVE THE PATIENCE OF A SAINT, YOU MIGHT ATTACK THE DOTS WITH EMBROIDERY COTTON AND FRENCH KNOTS.

3. PLACE PIECES #**2** ON PIECES #**3**. STITCH AROUND PETALS.

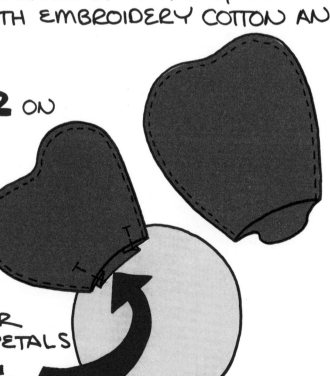

4. FOLD THE LARGER BACK PETALS. PIN PETALS AROUND PIECE #**4**.

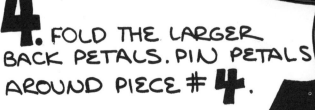

5. FLIP OVER THE PINNED FLOWER. STITCH AROUND #**4.**

(ON THIS SIDE YOU CAN STITCH AN EVEN LINE AROUND THE CIRCLE.)

6. PIN POLKA DOTTED PIECE TO FRONT OF FLOWER. BASTE SO THAT BASTING STITCHES ON FRONT COINCIDE WITH MACHINE STITCHES ON BACK. LEAVE ONE PETAL SECTION OPEN FOR STUFFING. STITCH.

7. STUFF. STITCH OPENING CLOSED.

8. PIN SOCK TO BACK OF FLOWER START AT CENTER OF TOE AND WORK AROUND BOTH SIDES. STRETCH THE SOCK AS YOU PIN. (THE HEEL WILL BECOME A MOUTH, SO YOU ARE PINNING THE OPPOSITE OR ANKLE SIDE TO THE FLOWER.) WHEN YOU GET TO THE FRONT ANKLE, FLIP THE SOCK UP SO YOU CAN PIN THE SINGLE LAYER MORE EASILY.

9. HAND STITCH THE SOCK TO THE FELT.

10. INVENT SOME EYES AND SEW THEM ON.

FLOWER B
BLACK-EYED SUSAN

YOU WILL NEED:
POLYESTER FIBER FILL
ONE 100% STRETCH NYLON
   CHILD'S KNEE SOCK-SIZE 6-7
FELT

1. PIN TWELVE STAMENS (#**10**) TO #**5**.

2. STARTING ¼" FROM END OF PIECE #**5**, STITCH #**6** TO #**5** BY SLOWLY TURNING THE CIRCLE. ¼" OF PIECE #**5** SHOULD BE LEFT OVER AT THE OTHER END. STITCH DOWN SIDE.

3. PIN BLACK EYE ON PIECE #**4**. LEAVE AN OPENING FOR STUFFING. STITCH. STUFF. STITCH OPENING CLOSED.

4. PLACE PIECES #**7** ON PIECES #**8**. STITCH PETALS TOGETHER. FOLD LARGER BACK OF PETAL.

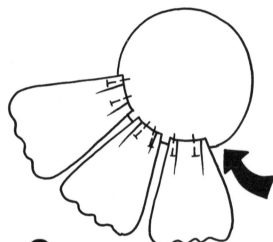

5. PIN RIGHT SIDE OF PETALS TO BACK OF EYE.

6. PLACE BACK OF EYE AND PINNED PETALS OVER PATTERN PIECE #**9**. USING ZIPPER FOOT, MACHINE STITCH AROUND EYE. FOLLOW EXISTING LINE OF STITCHING.

7. TRIM PATTERN PIECE #**9** TO MATCH #**4**. FOLLOW DIRECTIONS AS FOR **FLOWER A** STEPS **8 - 10.**

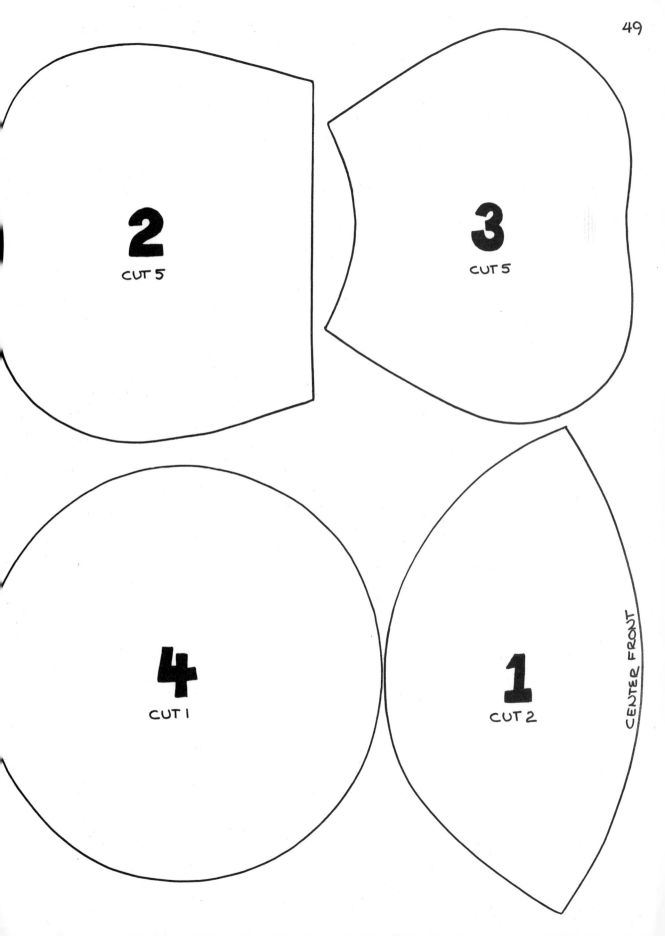

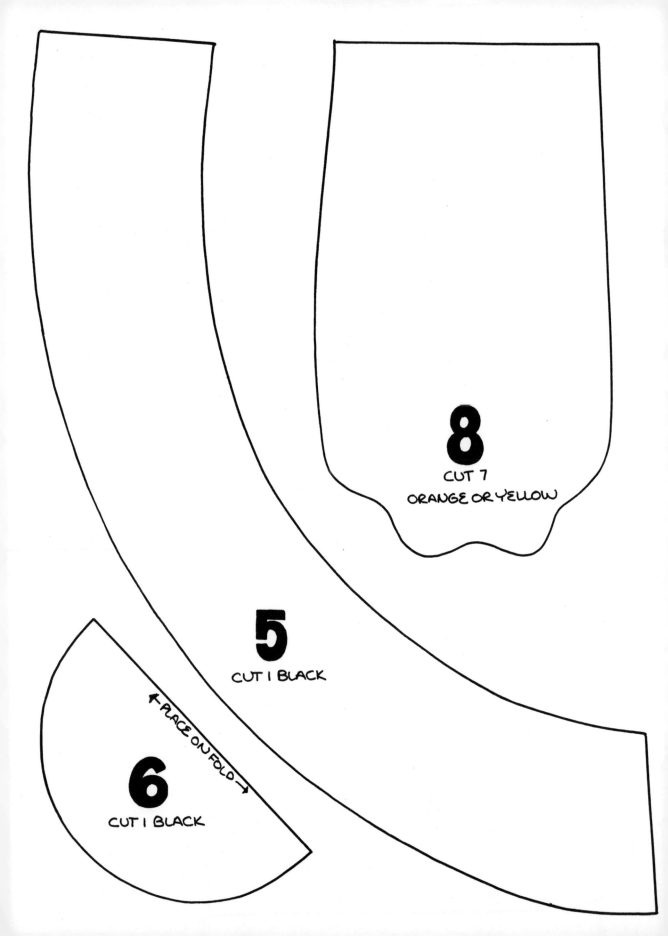

8
CUT 7
ORANGE OR YELLOW

5
CUT 1 BLACK

← PLACE ON FOLD →

6
CUT 1 BLACK

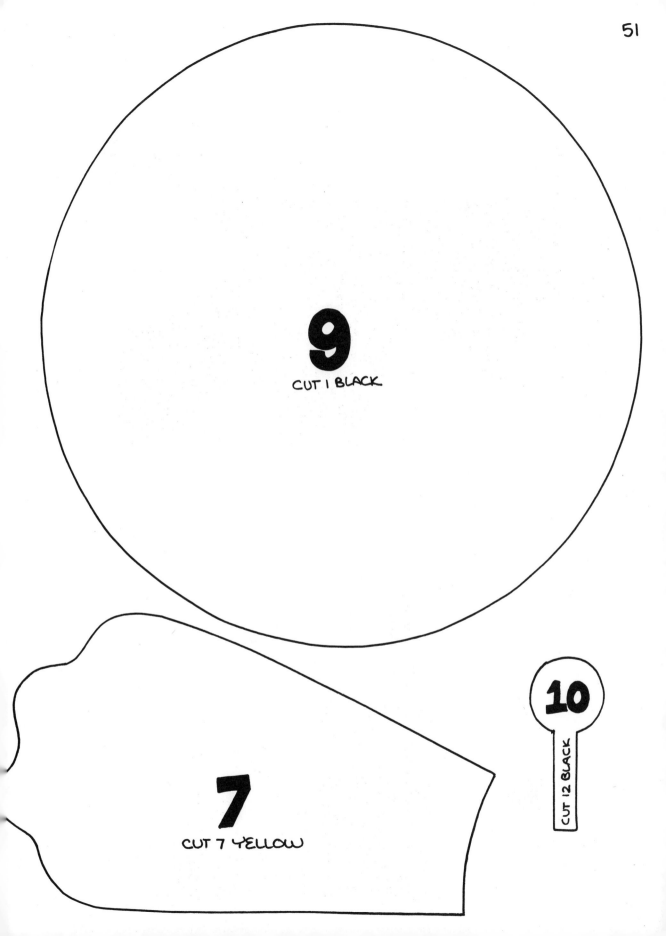

9

CUT 1 BLACK

7

CUT 7 YELLOW

10

CUT 12 BLACK

YELLOW-BILLED RED-WINGED BLACKBIRD PUPPET

YOU WILL NEED:
POLYESTER FIBER FILL
12" x 39" BLACK FELT
11" x 17" YELLOW FELT
SCRAPS OF RED AND WHITE FELT

1. STITCH RED PATCHES (#**1**) TO UPPER WINGS (#**2**).

STITCH YELLOW STRIPES (#**3**) OVER RED PATCHES.

2. STITCH PIECES # **4** TOGETHER.

STITCH UPPER BEAK (#**5**) TO ONE HALF OF INSIDE OF MOUTH.

STITCH LOWER BEAK (#**6**) TO OTHER HALF OF INSIDE OF MOUTH.

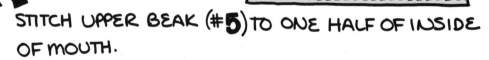

3. PIN AND STITCH UPPER BEAK TO HEAD OF BODY FRONT (#**7**). PIN AND STITCH LOWER BEAK.

5. TURN HEAD OVER AND CUT HOLE ¼" FROM STITCHING LINE.

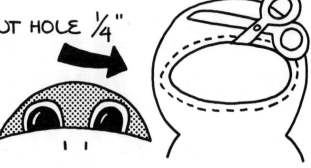

6. STITCH EYES TO FACE. DRAW NOSTRILS ON BEAK.

7. STITCH CENTER FRONTS OF PIECES #**9** TOGETHER.

8. PIN AND STITCH BELLY AND LEGS TO BODY FRONT. LEAVE OPENING FOR STUFFING. STUFF BELLY. STITCH OPENING CLOSED.

9. STITCH BLACK WINGS TO BODY FRONT (#**7**) AND WINGS WITH RED PATCH AND YELLOW STRIPE TO BODY BACK (#**8**). DO THE BACK FIRST AND THEN LAYING THE FRONT ON THE BACK, MATCH THE ANGLE OF THE WINGS BEFORE PINNING AND STITCHING.

10. STITCH FRONT AND BACK TOGETHER DOWN SIDE FROM YELLOW STRIPE ON WING TO TAIL-FEATHER.

11. STUFF WINGS TO YELLOW STRIPE.

12. STITCH ACROSS YELLOW STRIPES AND CLOSE WINGS ACROSS RED PATCHES.

13. STITCH AROUND HEAD.

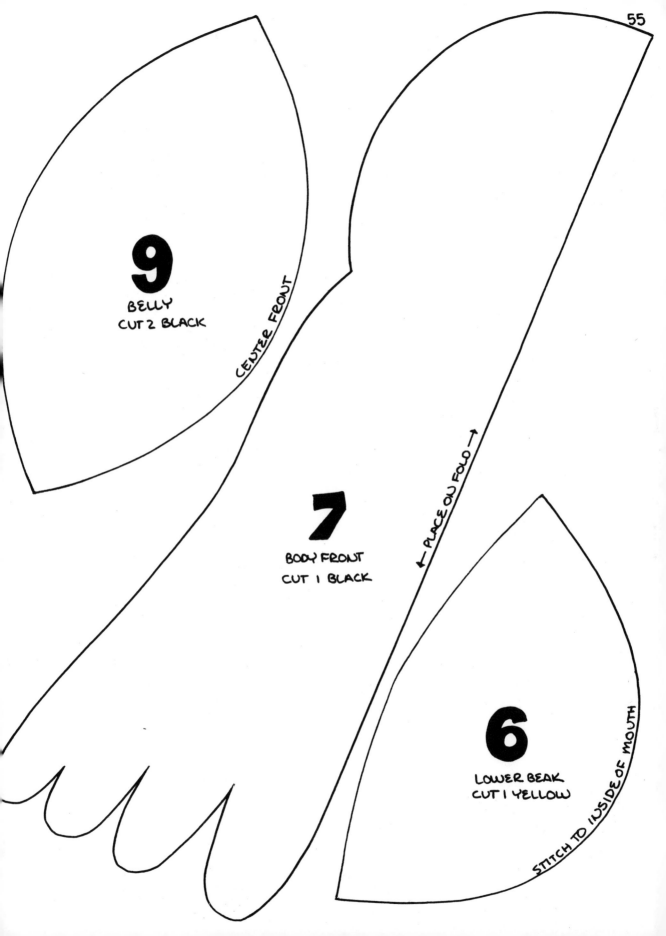

9

BELLY
CUT 2 BLACK

CENTER FRONT

7

BODY FRONT
CUT 1 BLACK

← PLACE ON FOLD →

6

LOWER BEAK
CUT 1 YELLOW

STITCH TO INSIDE OF MOUTH

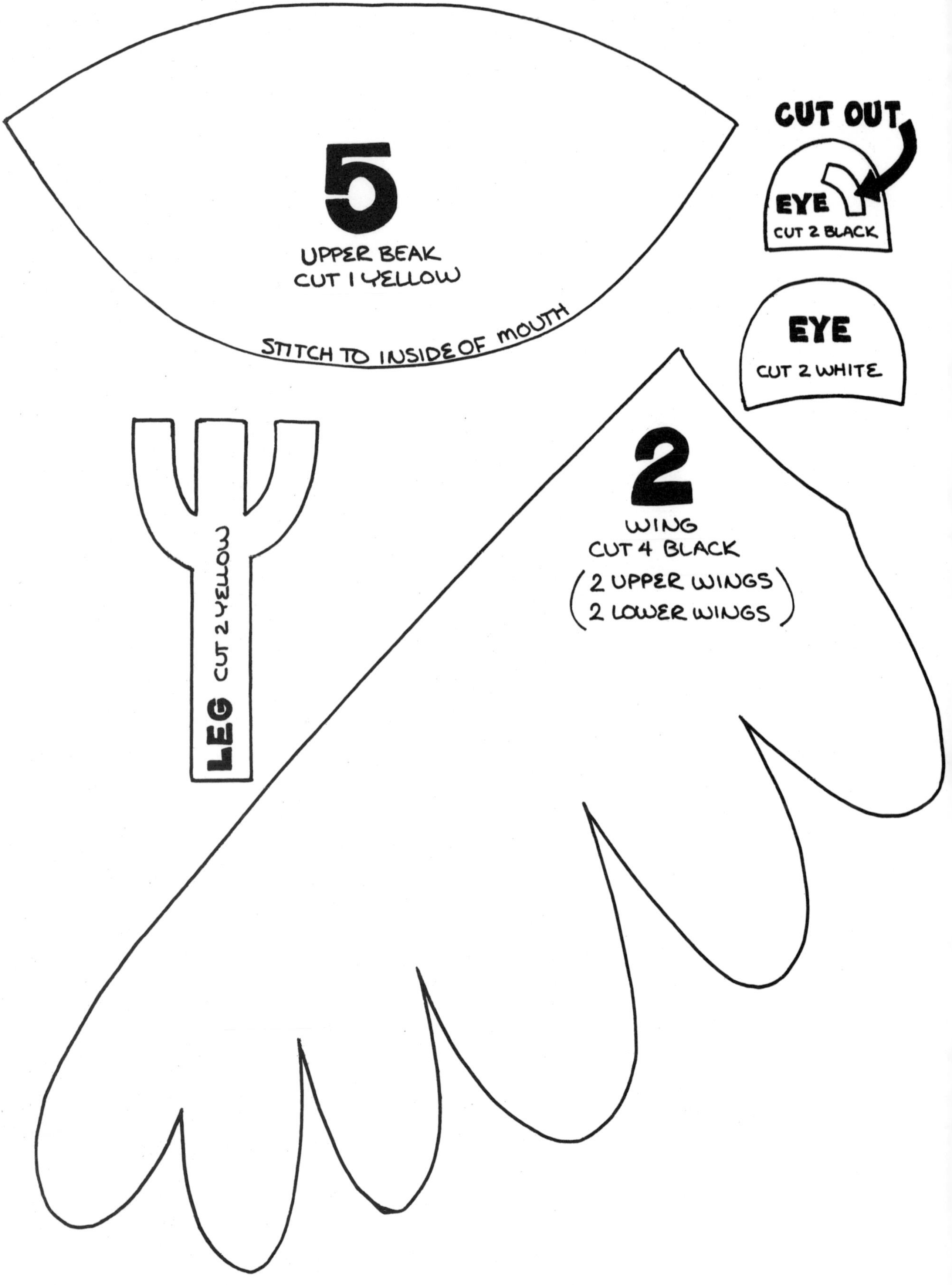

5

UPPER BEAK
CUT 1 YELLOW

STITCH TO INSIDE OF MOUTH

CUT OUT

EYE
CUT 2 BLACK

EYE
CUT 2 WHITE

LEG CUT 2 YELLOW

2

WING
CUT 4 BLACK
(2 UPPER WINGS)
(2 LOWER WINGS)

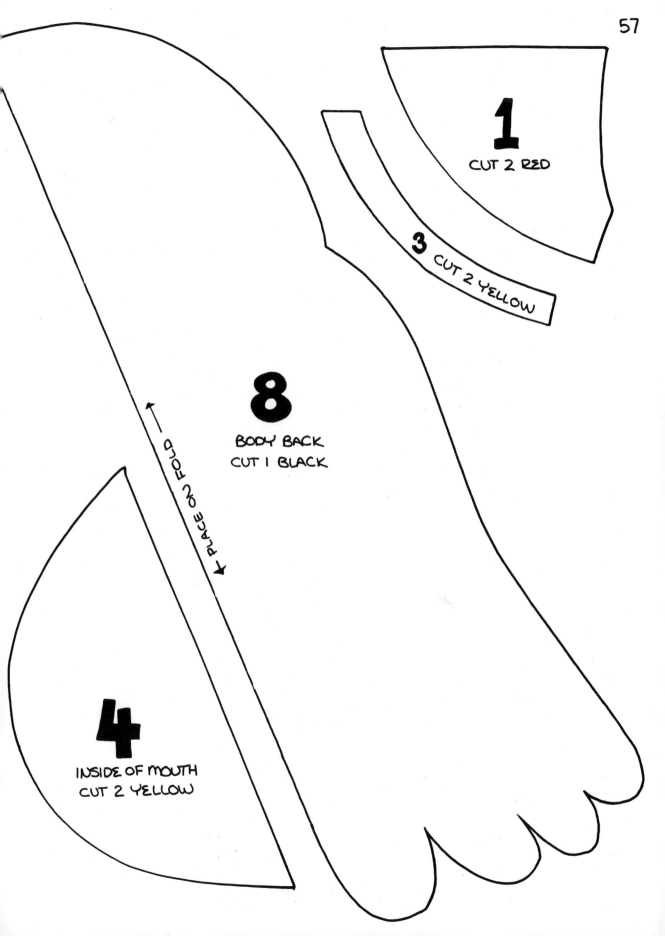

1

CUT 2 RED

3 CUT 2 YELLOW

8

BODY BACK
CUT 1 BLACK

← PLACE ON FOLD →

4

INSIDE OF MOUTH
CUT 2 YELLOW

KINGFISHER PUPPET

YOU WILL NEED:
   POLYESTER FIBER FILL
   38" x 9" BLUE FELT
   6" x 9" WHITE FELT
   11½" x 5" BLACK FELT
   BROWN, RED, PINK SCRAPS
   WHITE PAINT

1. STITCH RED PATTERN #**1** ON PIECES #**2**.

2. STITCH CENTER FRONTS OF PIECES #**2** TOGETHER.

3. STITCH WHITE CHIN PATTERN (#**3**) TO BODY FRONT (#**4**).

4. INSERT TONGUE (#**5**) BETWEEN PIECES #**6**. STITCH TOGETHER, THUS FORMING INSIDE OF MOUTH.

5. STITCH UPPER BEAK (#**7**) TO ONE HALF OF INSIDE OF MOUTH.

6. STITCH LOWER BEAK (#**8**) TO OTHER HALF OF INSIDE OF MOUTH.

7. PIN AND STITCH UPPER BEAK TO BODY FRONT (#**4**). PIN AND STITCH LOWER BEAK. TURN OVER AND CUT HOLE ¼" FROM STITCHING LINE.

8. STITCH EYES TO FACE.

9. PIN AND STITCH BELLY AND LEGS TO BODY. LEAVE OPENING FOR STUFFING. STUFF AND STITCH OPENING CLOSED.

10. STITCH UPPER WINGS TO BODY BACK (#**10**).

11. STITCH LOWER WINGS TO BODY FRONT. MAKE SURE FRONT AND BACK OF BIRD MATCH.

12. STITCH FRONT AND BACK TOGETHER. STITCH FROM **A** AROUND WING AND DOWN SIDE TO **B**.

13. STUFF WINGS TO **A**. STITCH ACROSS WING (DOTTED LINE INDICATED ON PATTERN) AND CLOSE WING.

14. STITCH AROUND HEAD. PAINT WHITE DOTS ON WINGS/TAIL.

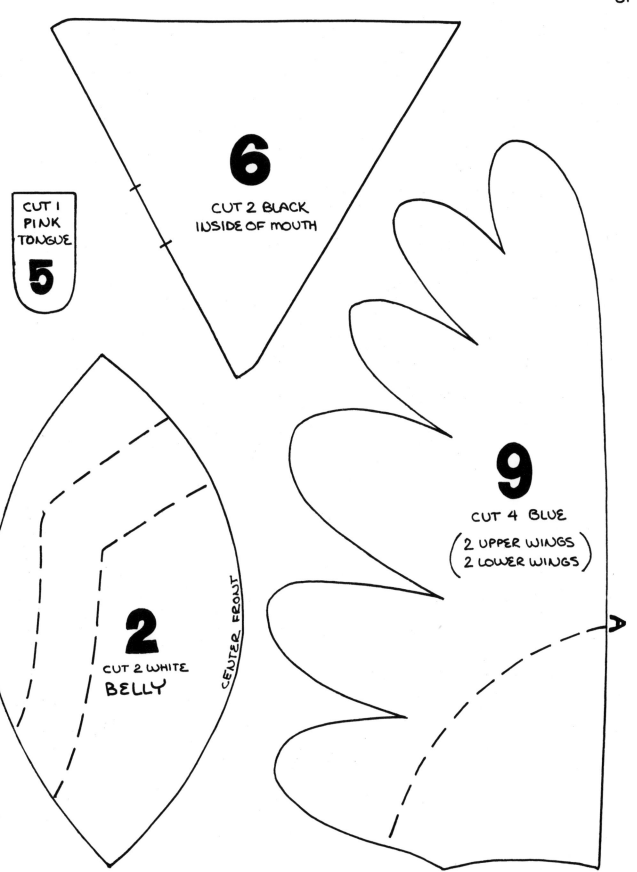

61

6

CUT 2 BLACK
INSIDE OF MOUTH

CUT 1
PINK
TONGUE

5

9

CUT 4 BLUE

(2 UPPER WINGS)
(2 LOWER WINGS)

2

CUT 2 WHITE
BELLY

CENTER FRONT

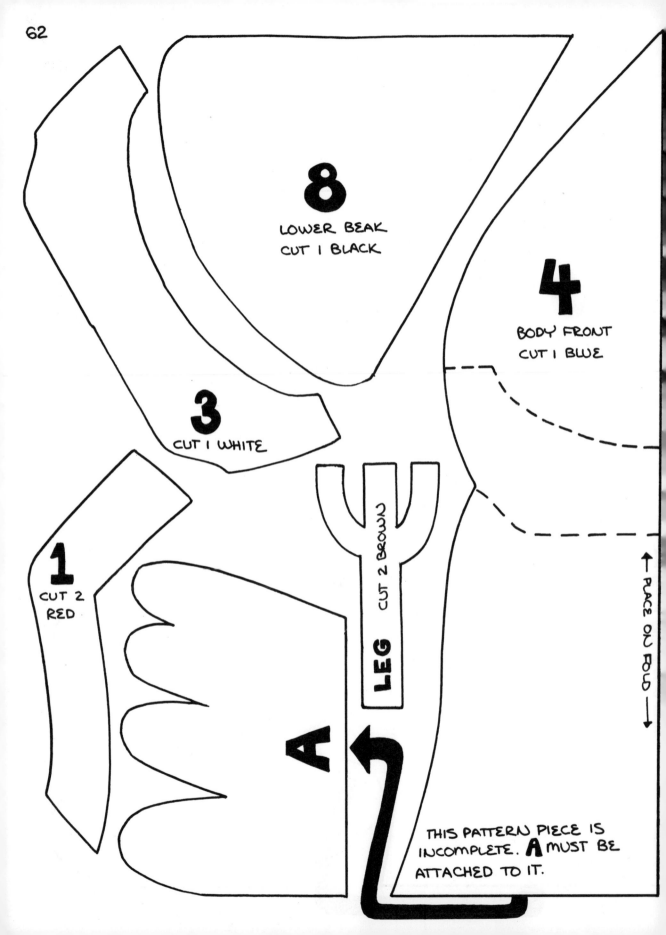

8
LOWER BEAK
CUT 1 BLACK

4
BODY FRONT
CUT 1 BLUE

3
CUT 1 WHITE

1
CUT 2
RED

LEG CUT 2 BROWN

PLACE ON FOLD

A

THIS PATTERN PIECE IS
INCOMPLETE. **A** MUST BE
ATTACHED TO IT.

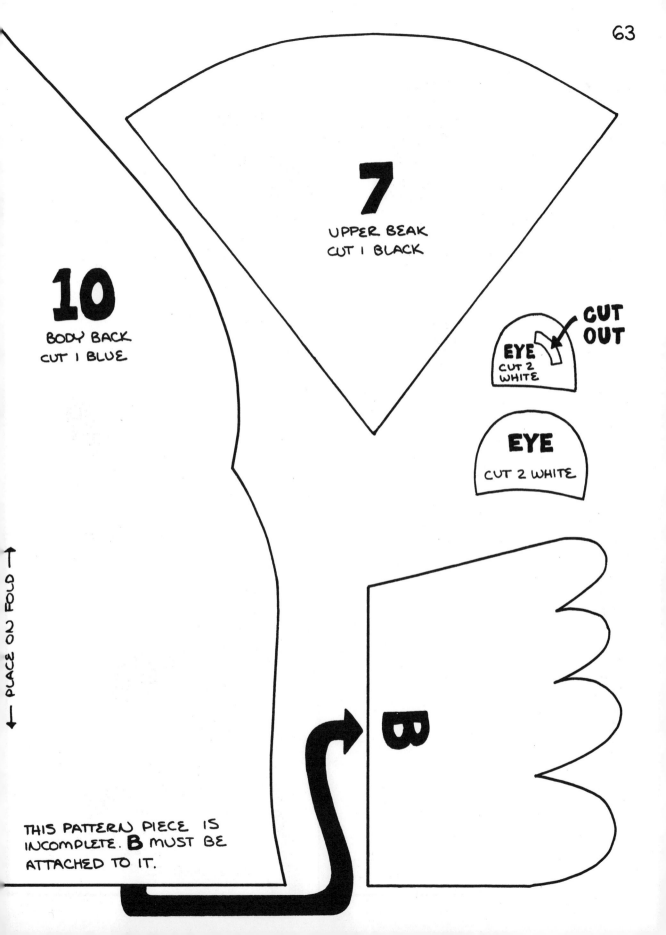

7

UPPER BEAK
CUT 1 BLACK

10

BODY BACK
CUT 1 BLUE

CUT
OUT

EYE
CUT 2
WHITE

EYE

CUT 2 WHITE

← PLACE ON FOLD →

B

THIS PATTERN PIECE IS
INCOMPLETE. **B** MUST BE
ATTACHED TO IT.

GIRAFFE PUPPET

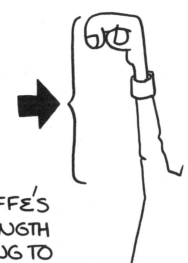

THE LENGTH OF THE GIRAFFE'S NECK DEPENDS ON THE LENGTH OF THE ARM THAT IS GOING TO FIT IN IT. MEASURE FROM THE KNUCKLES TO THE BEGINNING OF THE SHOULDER AND LENGTHEN PIECES #**1** AND #**2** TO THAT MEASUREMENT.

YOU WILL NEED:
    FOR A 22" PUPPET
23"x1" FAKE FUR
23"x18" WHITE FELT
8½" x 37" BROWN FELT
SCRAPS OF PINK AND
    BLACK FELT

1. STITCH STRIP OF FAKE FUR DOWN MIDDLE OF GIRAFFE BACK (#**1**).

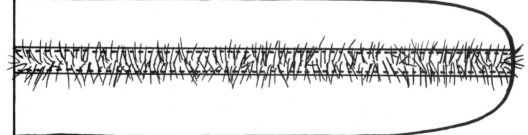

2. CUT OUT BROWN SPOTS AND STITCH ON BACK.

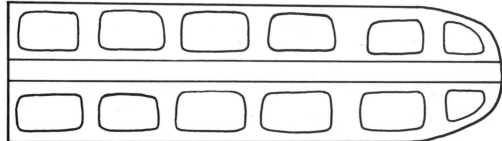

66

3. STITCH PIECES **A, B, C, D** ON FACE. YOU MAY PREFER GLUING THE SMALL PIECES.

4. CUT OUT SOME NOSTRILS AND STITCH TO FACE.

5. STITCH EYES ON FACE.

STITCH ¼" × 1" STRIP OF FAKE FUR TO EYELID. (RIGHT SIDE OF FUR TO WRONG SIDE OF EYELID.)

STITCH EYELIDS OVER EYES.

6. STITCH HALVES OF TONGUE TOGETHER (#**6**). STUFF.

7. STITCH PINK INNER EARS (#**7**) TO WHITE EARS (#**8**).

8. STITCH WHITE EARS TO BROWN EARS.

FRONT   BACK

9. STITCH AROUND HORNS (#**9**). STUFF.

10. PLACE TONGUE BETWEEN PIECES #**10** AND #**11**. STITCH ACROSS.

11. STITCH # **12** TO # **11**.

12. STITCH THE FACE TO # **10**.

13. STITCH ENTIRE FACE TO BODY FRONT. (# **2**). STITCH FROM **A** (CORNER OF MOUTH) TO **B** (OTHER CORNER OF MOUTH). LIFT THREAD. STITCH FROM **B** TO **A**. THE PLACEMENT OF THE FACE IS OUTLINED ON PATTERN # **2**.

14. FLIP FACE OVER AND CUT OUT A CIRCLE ¼" FROM STITCHING LINE.

15. STITCH BROWN SPOTS ON BODY FRONT.

16. FOLD OVER EARS AT BOTTOM. PIN TO # **1**.

PIN HORNS ON # **1**.

17. PIN FRONT AND BACK OF PUPPET TOGETHER. STITCH AROUND PUPPET.

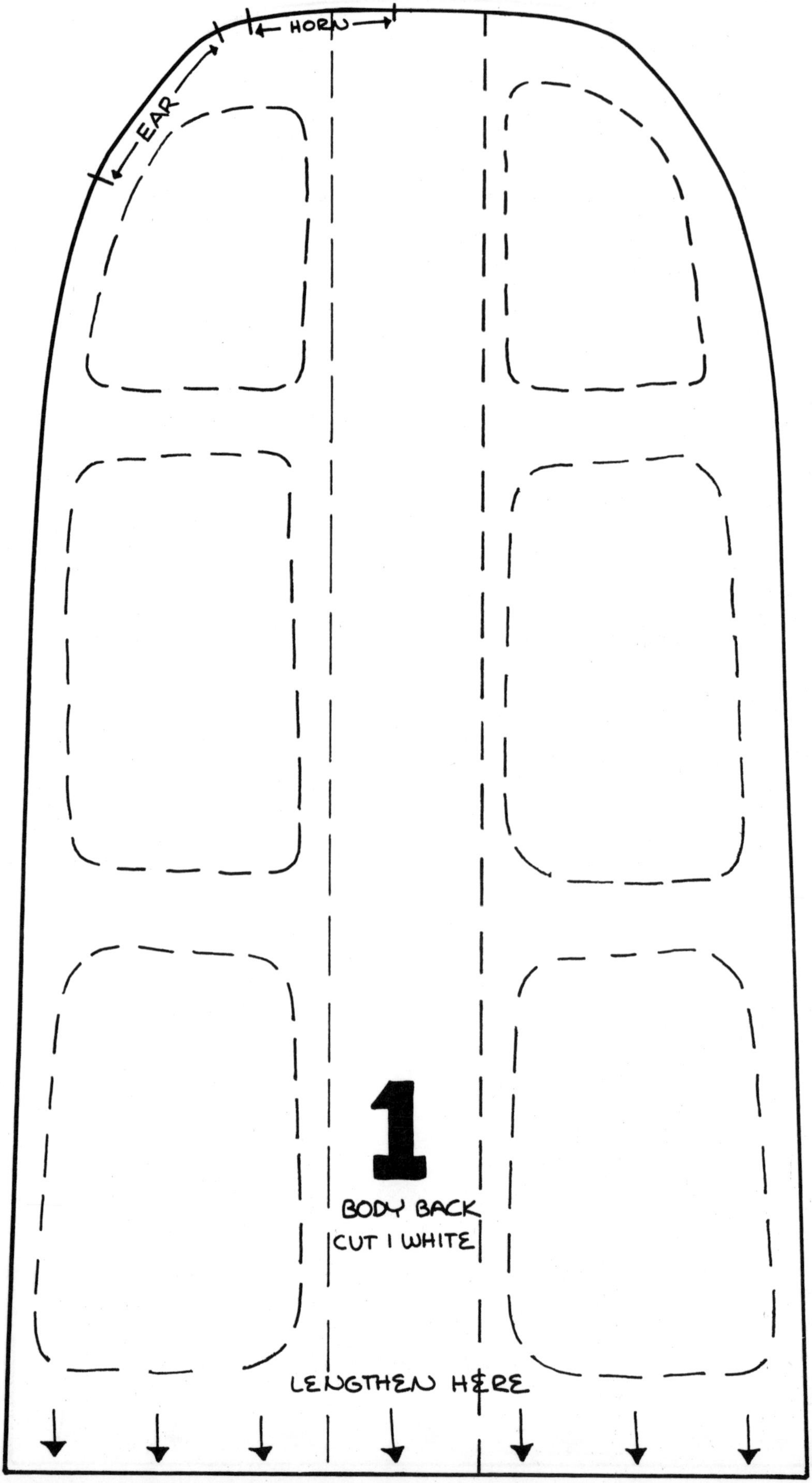

68

EAR

HORN

1

BODY BACK

CUT 1 WHITE

LENGTHEN HERE

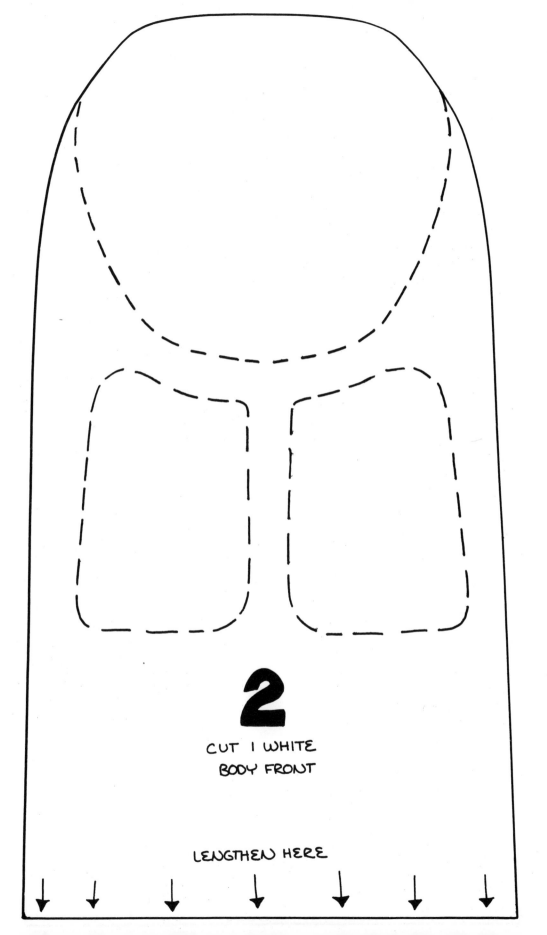

2

CUT 1 WHITE
BODY FRONT

LENGTHEN HERE

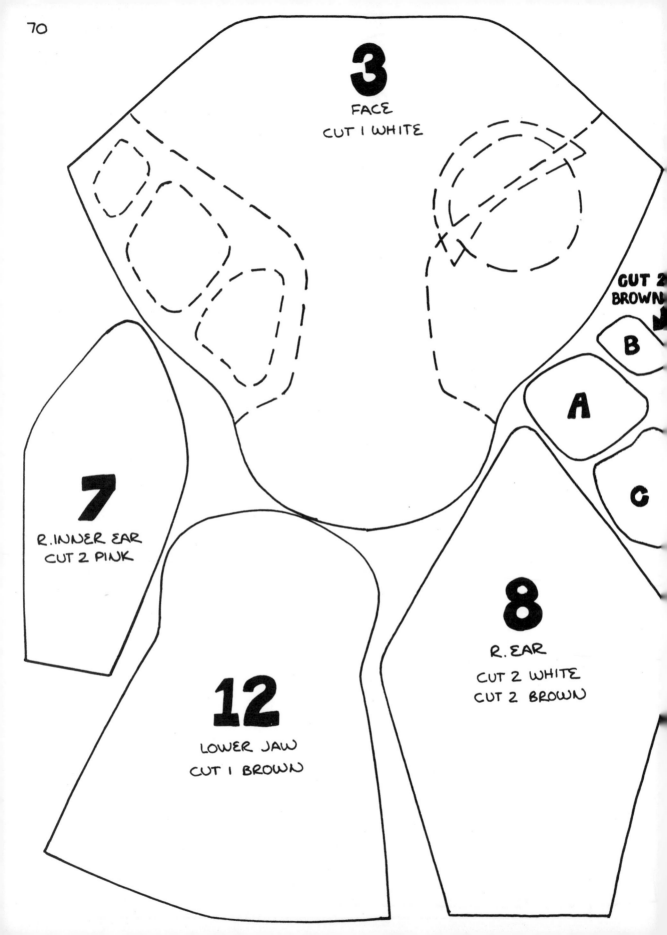

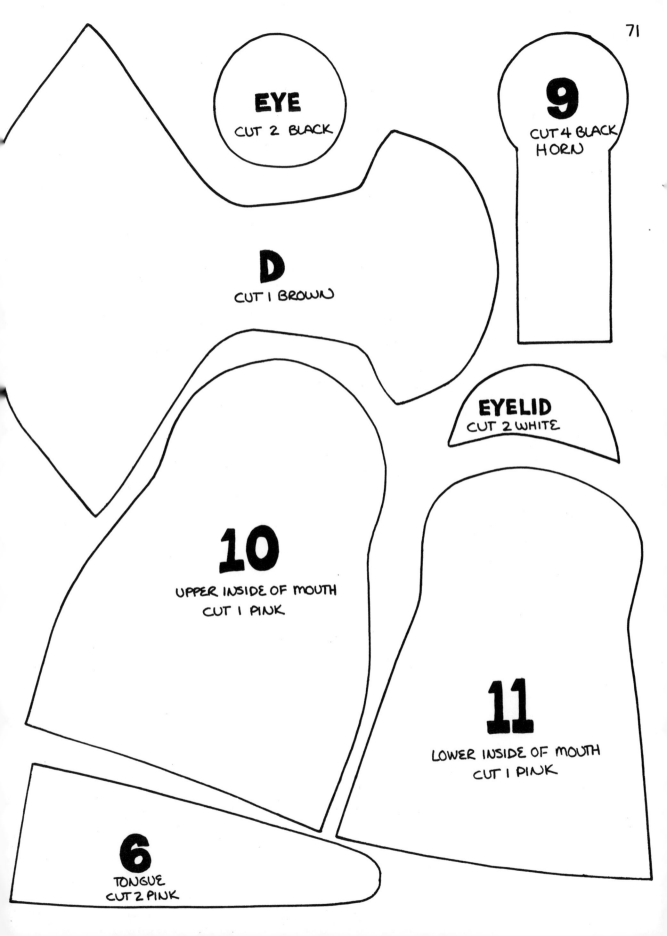

EYE
CUT 2 BLACK

9
CUT 4 BLACK
HORN

D
CUT 1 BROWN

EYELID
CUT 2 WHITE

10
UPPER INSIDE OF MOUTH
CUT 1 PINK

11
LOWER INSIDE OF MOUTH
CUT 1 PINK

6
TONGUE
CUT 2 PINK

BABY BABY DOLL

1. HAND EMBROIDER FACE (#**8**) AND BELLY BUTTON (#**7**).

2. STITCH HAIR ON TOP OF HEAD (#**1**). SEW 1½" PIECES OF YARN IN SIX ROWS ACROSS PATE.

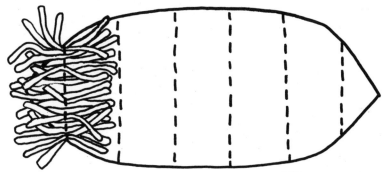

3. STITCH AROUND EARS. STUFF LOOSELY. STITCH OVER STUFFING ALONG DOTTED LINES INDICATED ON PATTERN.

4.

STITCH TOP OF HEAD (#**1**) FROM **A** to **B** ALONG FRONT AND BACK OF HEAD (#**8**).

(#**1** WILL HAVE HAIR ON IT. AVOID STITCHING ACROSS YARN.)

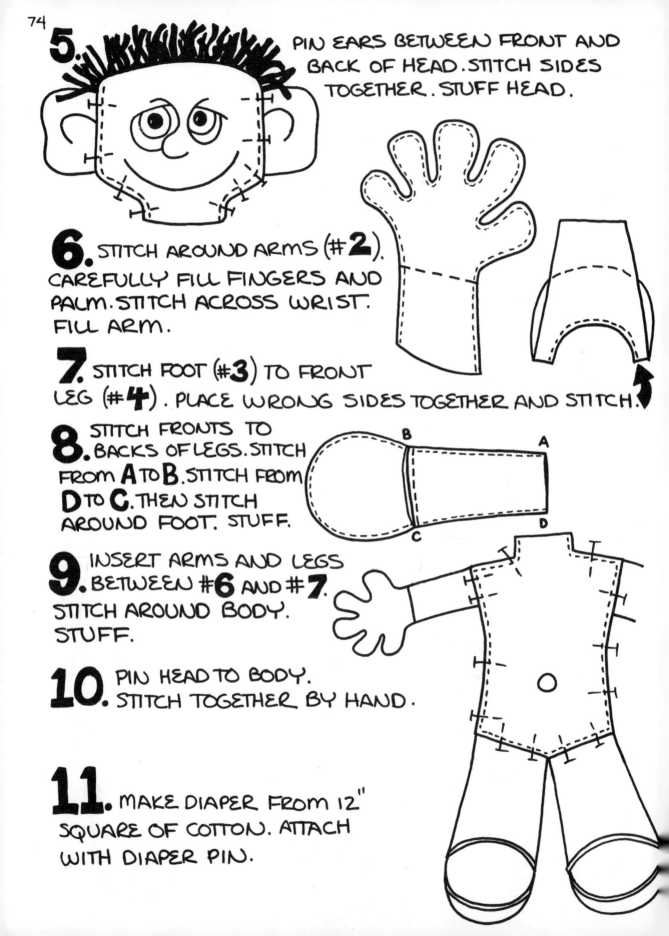

5. PIN EARS BETWEEN FRONT AND BACK OF HEAD. STITCH SIDES TOGETHER. STUFF HEAD.

6. STITCH AROUND ARMS (#**2**). CAREFULLY FILL FINGERS AND PALM. STITCH ACROSS WRIST. FILL ARM.

7. STITCH FOOT (#**3**) TO FRONT LEG (#**4**). PLACE WRONG SIDES TOGETHER AND STITCH.

8. STITCH FRONTS TO BACKS OF LEGS. STITCH FROM **A** TO **B**. STITCH FROM **D** TO **C**. THEN STITCH AROUND FOOT. STUFF.

9. INSERT ARMS AND LEGS BETWEEN #**6** AND #**7**. STITCH AROUND BODY. STUFF.

10. PIN HEAD TO BODY. STITCH TOGETHER BY HAND.

11. MAKE DIAPER FROM 12" SQUARE OF COTTON. ATTACH WITH DIAPER PIN.

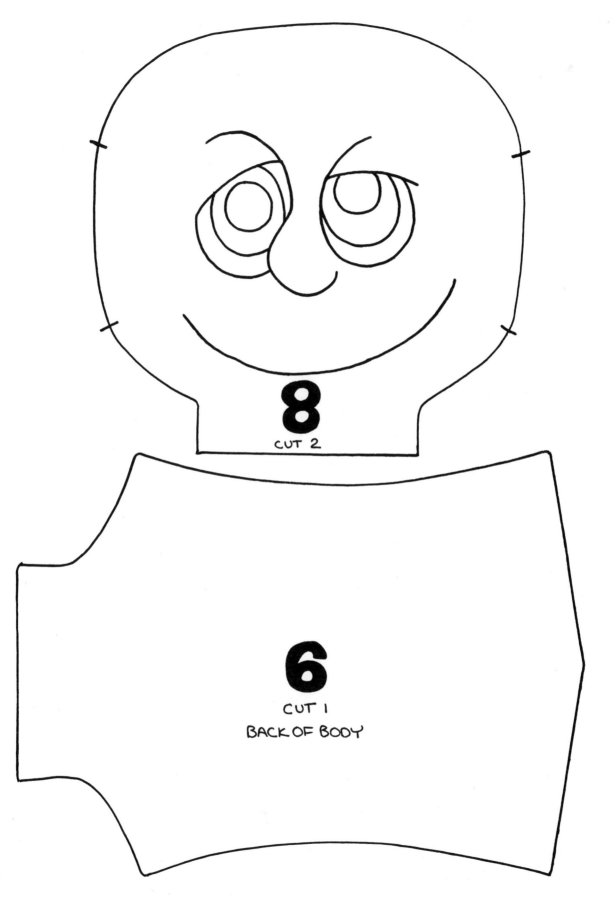

8

CUT 2

6

CUT 1

BACK OF BODY

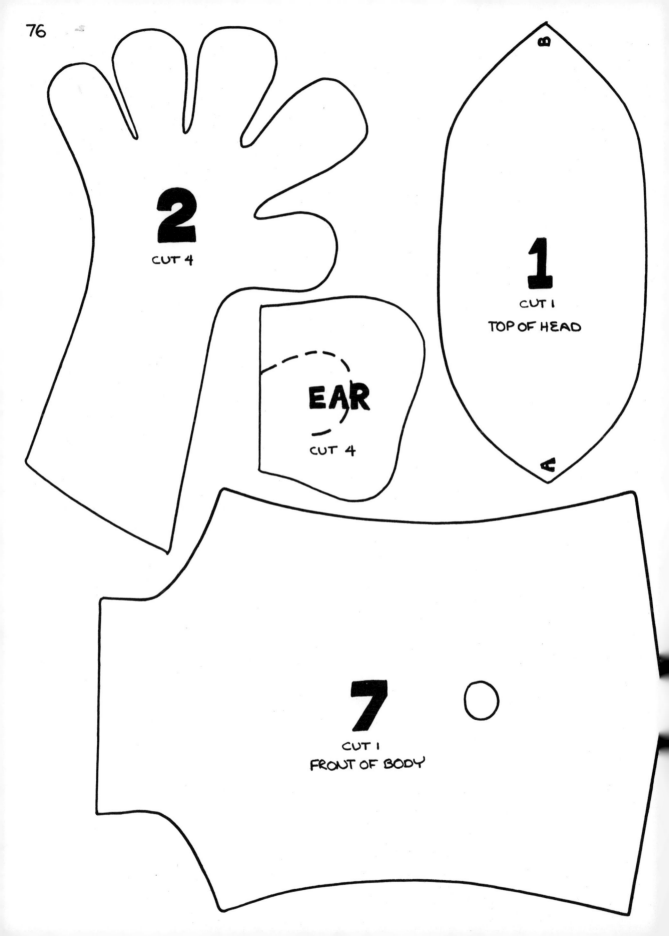

2

CUT 4

1

CUT 1

TOP OF HEAD

EAR

CUT 4

7

CUT 1

FRONT OF BODY

B

C

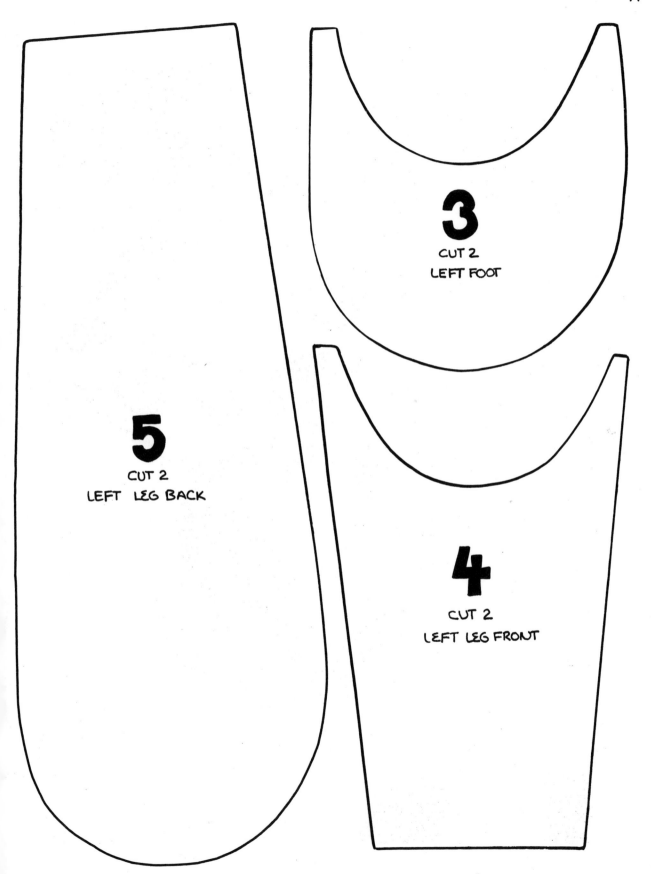

5

CUT 2

LEFT LEG BACK

3

CUT 2

LEFT FOOT

4

CUT 2

LEFT LEG FRONT

LEOPARD FROG

YOU WILL NEED:
POLYESTER FIBER FILL
16"x37" GREEN FELT
SCRAPS OF BLACK, WHITE,
    PINK AND DARK GREEN FELT
SINGER "DOT" SNAPPERS
SCRAP OF INTERFACING

1. ATTACH SNAPS TO FROG THIGHS AND BACKS. USE ONE EXTRA LAYER OF FELT AND ONE LAYER OF INTER- FACING.

2. STITCH TOGETHER BACK SEAMS.

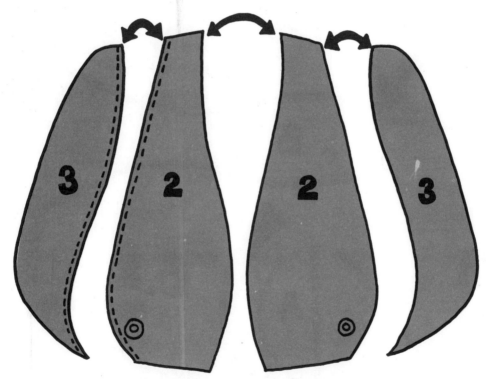

3. CUT OUT LOTS OF WIGGELY LEOPARD SPOTS. STITCH THEM ON THE OUTER THIGHS, OUTER LEGS AND THE BACK.

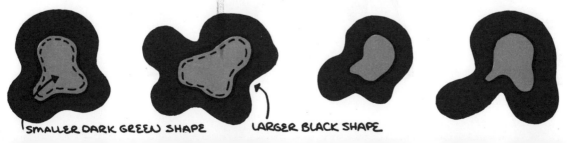

SMALLER DARK GREEN SHAPE   LARGER BLACK SHAPE

4. STITCH TOGETHER FRONTS AND BACKS OF BOTH SECTIONS OF LEGS. STUFF SECTION **A**. STUFF SECTION **B** (GET FILL INTO TOES) TO ANKLE. STITCH ACROSS. FILL TO TOP.

5. FIT SECTION **A** INTO SECTION **B**. STITCH.

6. STITCH CENTER FRONT OF PIECES #**4** TOGETHER

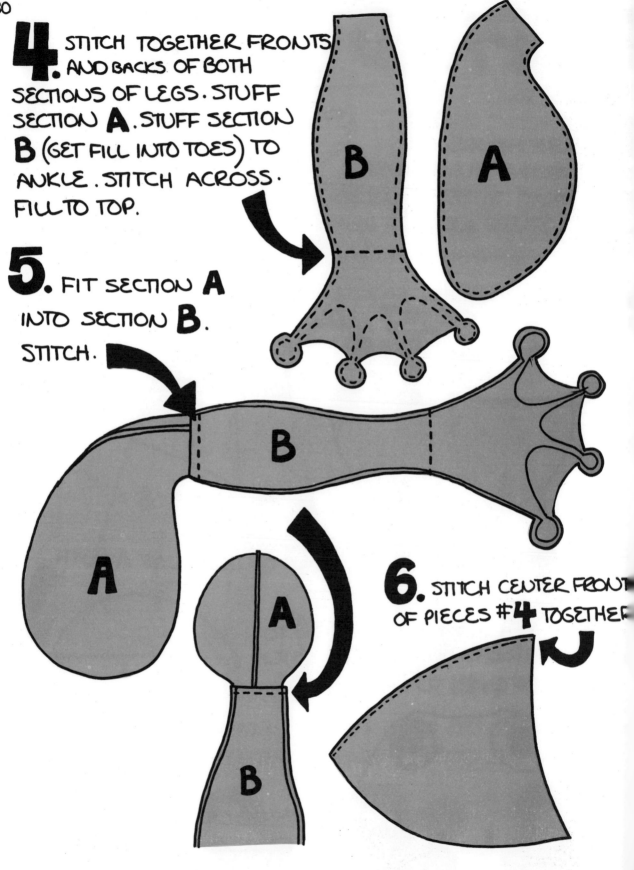

7. STITCH AROUND HANDS (#**5**).

8. STUFF HANDS. CAREFULLY FILL FINGERS. FILL PALM. STITCH ACROSS WRIST. STUFF REST OF ARM.

9. PLACE TONGUE (#**7**) BETWEEN INSIDES OF MOUTH (#**6**). STITCH.

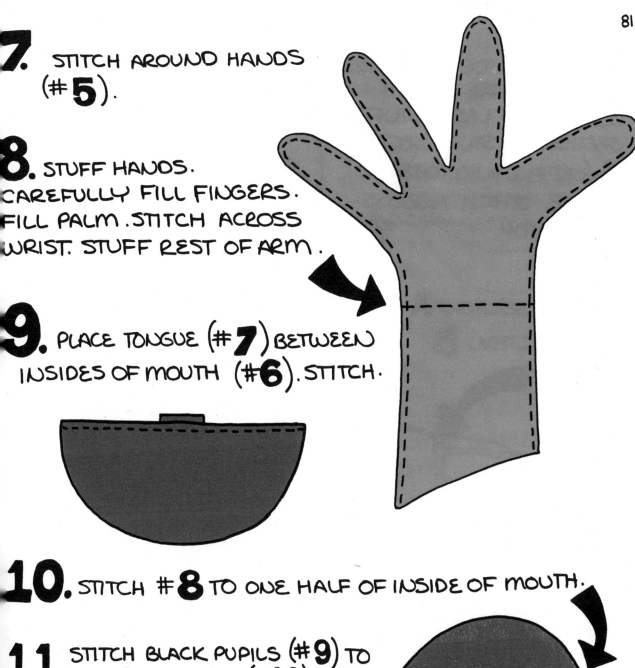

10. STITCH #**8** TO ONE HALF OF INSIDE OF MOUTH.

11. STITCH BLACK PUPILS (#**9**) TO WHITES OF EYES (#**10**). STITCH WHITES OF EYES TO FACE (#**11**).

DRAW ON NOSTRILS WITH FELT TIP MARKER.

12. STITCH FACE TO OTHER HALF OF INSIDE OF MOUTH.

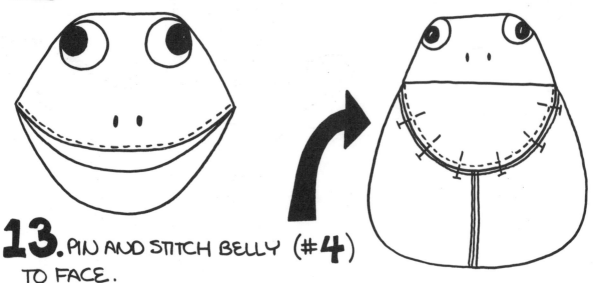

13. PIN AND STITCH BELLY (#**4**) TO FACE.

14. PIN ARMS TO WRONG SIDE OF #**4**. (POSITION INDICATED ON PATTERN PIECE #**4**.)

15. PIN FRONT OF FROG BODY TO BACK OF FROG BODY.

16. STITCH AROUND BODY. LEAVE OPENING AT REAR FOR STUFFING. STITCH FROM **A** TO **B** (CORNER OF MOUTH). LIFT THREAD. STITCH FROM **B** TO **C**. LIFT THREAD. STITCH FROM **C** TO **D**.

17. STUFF BODY. MACHINE STITCH OPENING CLOSED.

18. SNAP ON LEGS.

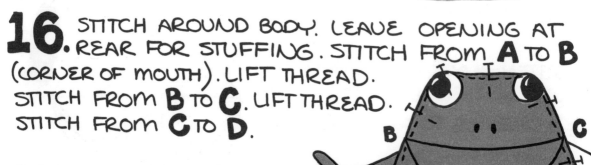

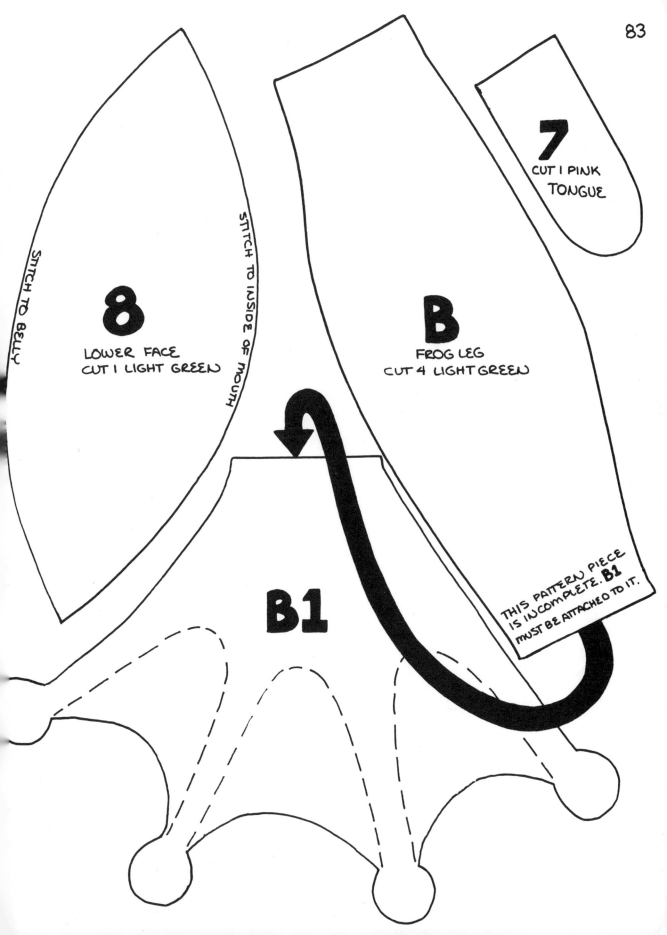

83

8
LOWER FACE
CUT 1 LIGHT GREEN

STITCH TO BELLY

STITCH TO INSIDE OF MOUTH

B
FROG LEG
CUT 4 LIGHT GREEN

7
CUT 1 PINK
TONGUE

B1

THIS PATTERN PIECE
IS INCOMPLETE. B1
MUST BE ATTACHED TO IT.

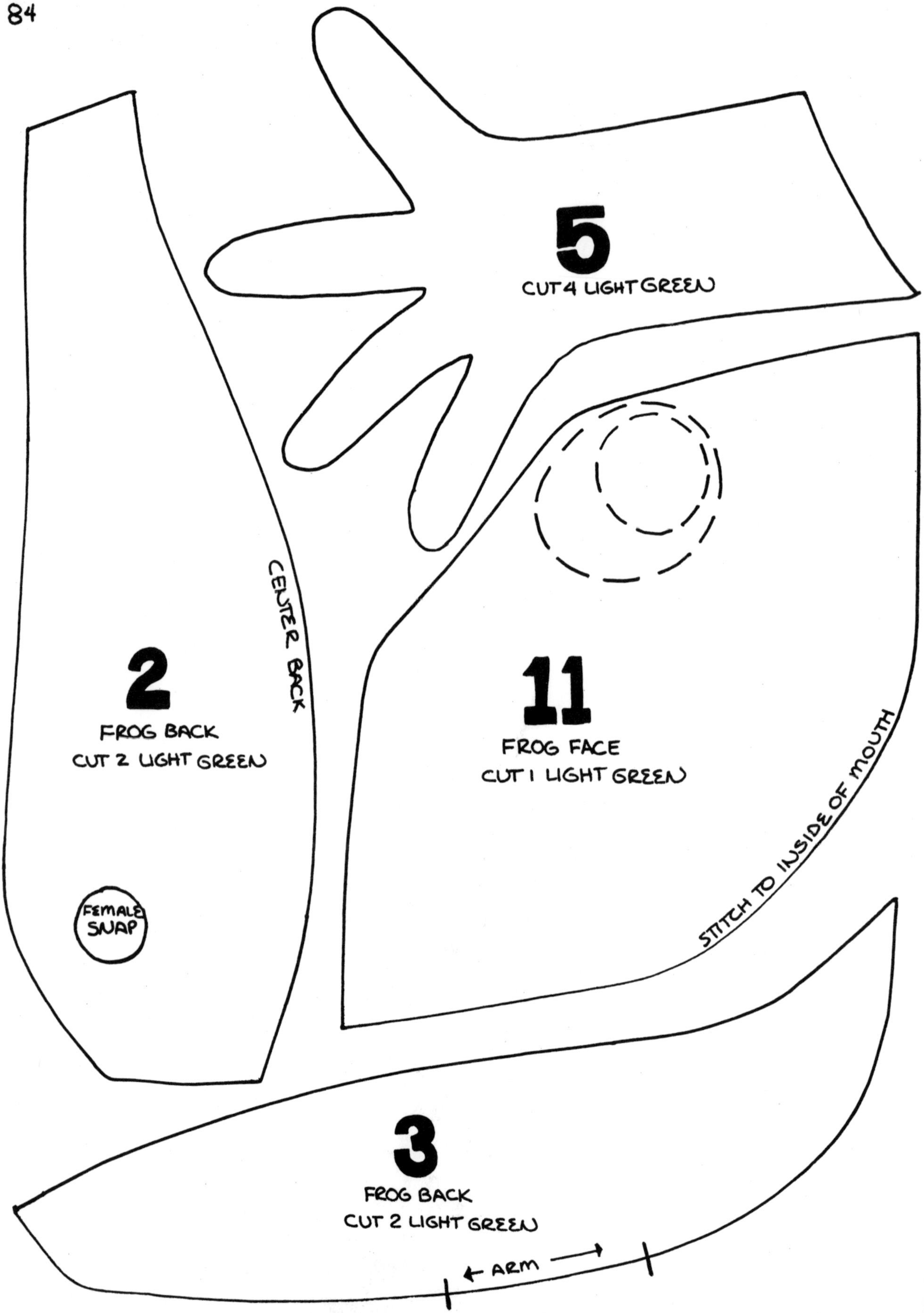

84

5

CUT 4 LIGHT GREEN

CENTER BACK

2

FROG BACK
CUT 2 LIGHT GREEN

FEMALE SNAP

11

FROG FACE
CUT 1 LIGHT GREEN

STITCH TO INSIDE OF MOUTH

3

FROG BACK
CUT 2 LIGHT GREEN

← ARM →

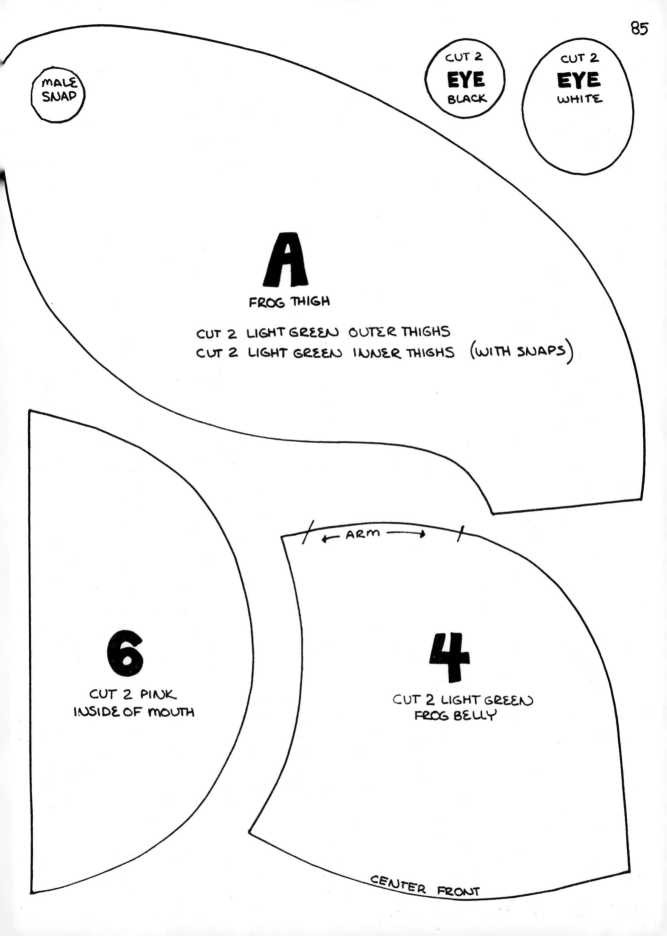

MALE SNAP

CUT 2 EYE BLACK

CUT 2 EYE WHITE

A

FROG THIGH

CUT 2 LIGHT GREEN OUTER THIGHS
CUT 2 LIGHT GREEN INNER THIGHS (WITH SNAPS)

6

CUT 2 PINK
INSIDE OF MOUTH

← ARM →

4

CUT 2 LIGHT GREEN
FROG BELLY

CENTER FRONT

TEDDY BEAR

YOU WILL NEED:
POLYESTER FIBER FILL
9"x36" BROWN FELT
SCRAPS OF PINK,
BLACK, WHITE FELT

1. STITCH DART IN LOWER FACE FRONT. (**#1**)

2. STITCH SNOUT (**#2**) AND NOSE (**#3**) TO **#1**. STITCH EYES TO FACE (**#6**).

3. STITCH FACE (**#6**) TO LOWER FACE FRONT (**#1**).

4. STITCH AROUND EARS. STUFF EARS.

5. PIN EARS TO FACE. PIN BACK OF HEAD (**#7**) TO FACE. STITCH.

6. STUFF MORE STUFFING THAN YOU THINK CAN POSSIBLY FIT IN HEAD TO MAKE SNOUT BULGE.

STITCH PAWS (**#9**) TO LEG FRONTS (**#10**).

7. STITCH **A, B, C, D, E** TO PIECES **#8**.

8. STITCH FRONTS TO BACKS OF LEGS. STITCH FROM **A** TO **B**. THEN STITCH FROM **C** TO **D**. THEN STITCH AROUND PAW. STUFF.

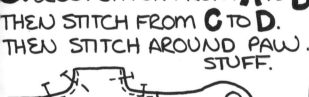

9. PIN LEGS BETWEEN BODY FRONT AND BACK. STITCH AROUND BODY.

10. STUFF BODY. DRAW ON BELLY BUTTON.

11. TURN BODY NECK IN ON ITSELF. SQUEEZE HEAD NECK INTO HOLE. PIN AND STITCH BY HAND.

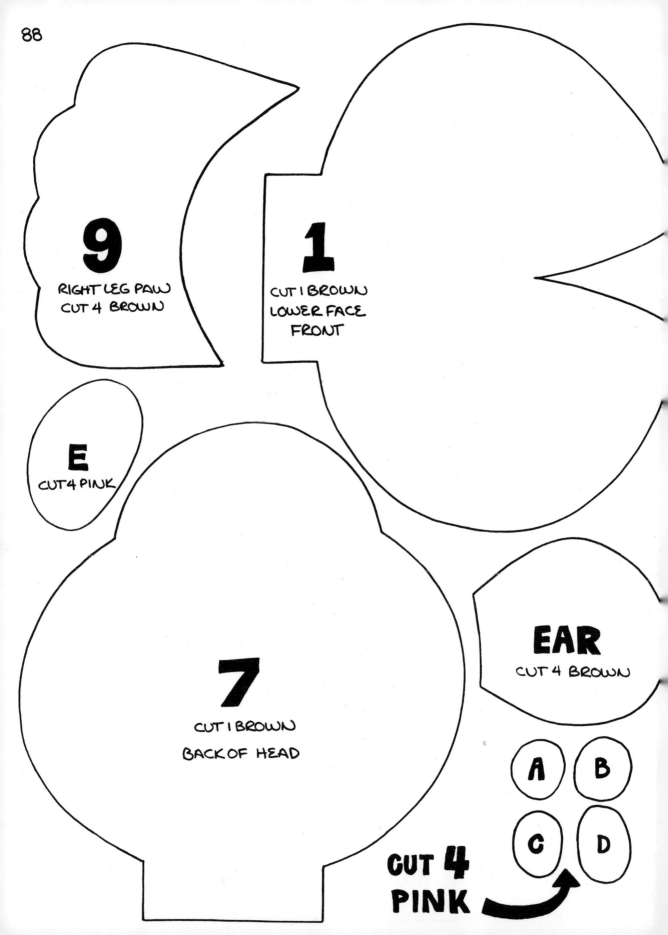

9

RIGHT LEG PAW
CUT 4 BROWN

1

CUT 1 BROWN
LOWER FACE
FRONT

E

CUT 4 PINK

7

CUT 1 BROWN

BACK OF HEAD

EAR

CUT 4 BROWN

Ⓐ   Ⓑ

Ⓒ   Ⓓ

CUT **4**
PINK

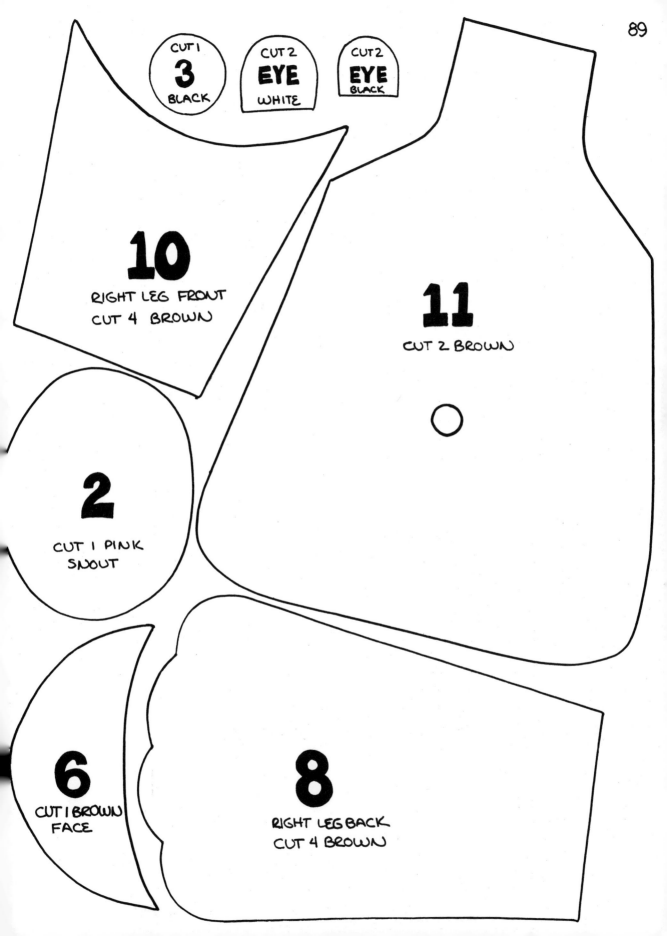

BAT

YOU WILL NEED:
37" x 6½" GREY FELT
POLYESTER FIBER FILL
66" OF 22 GAUGE WIRE
SCRAPS OF PINK, RED,
WHITE AND BLACK FELT

IF YOU WOULD LIKE TO SEE SOME INSPIRATIONAL REFERENCE MATERIAL BEFORE YOU START CONSTRUCTING THIS BAT, LOOK AT THE ARTICLE "BATS AREN'T ALL BAD" IN THE MAY, 1973 ISSUE OF THE NATIONAL GEOGRAPHIC.

1. STITCH TOGETHER CENTER FRONT SEAM OF BAT BODY (#**1**).

2.

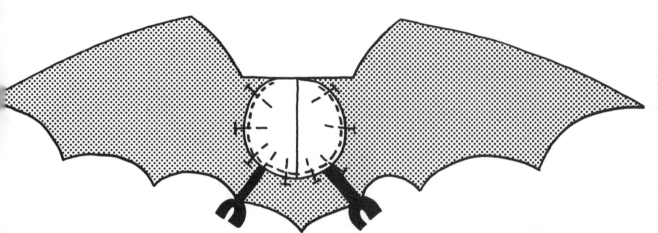

PIN BAT BODY TO LOWER WINGS. INSERT LEGS (#**2**). STITCH AROUND BODY. LEAVE A 1" OPENING AT NECK FOR STUFFING.

3. TURN OVER THE WINGS WITH BODY ATTACHED AND CUT AWAY THE GREY FELT ¼" INSIDE THE STITCHING LINE.

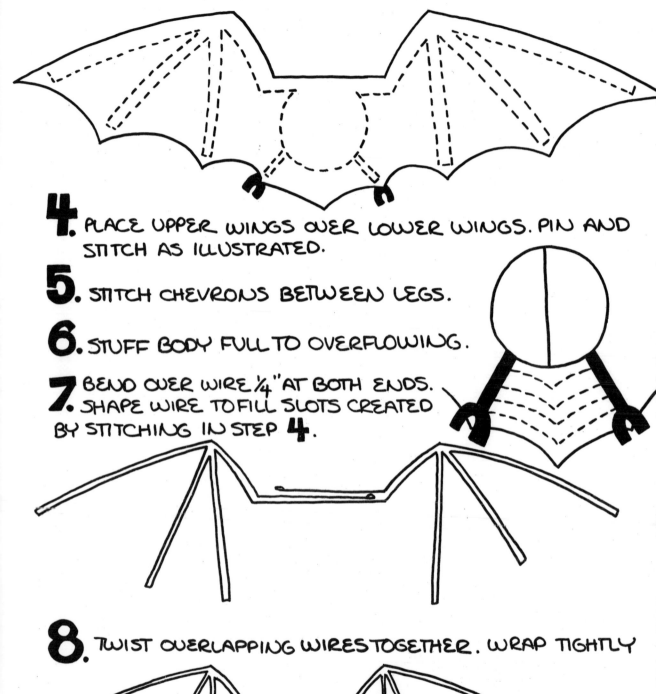

4. PLACE UPPER WINGS OVER LOWER WINGS. PIN AND STITCH AS ILLUSTRATED.

5. STITCH CHEVRONS BETWEEN LEGS.

6. STUFF BODY FULL TO OVERFLOWING.

7. BEND OVER WIRE ¼" AT BOTH ENDS. SHAPE WIRE TO FILL SLOTS CREATED BY STITCHING IN STEP **4.**

8. TWIST OVERLAPPING WIRES TOGETHER. WRAP TIGHTLY

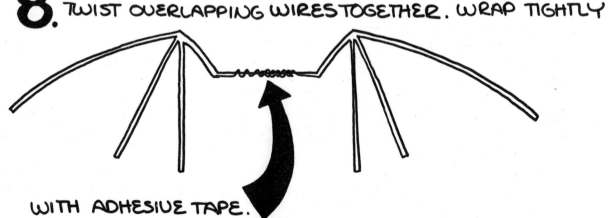

WITH ADHESIVE TAPE.

9. FIT WIRES INTO STITCHED SLOTS. SECURE WITH PINS ALONG TOPS OF WINGS.

10. STITCH TONGUE (#**4**) BETWEEN HALVES OF MOUTH (#**5**).

11. STITCH EYES, EARS AND EYELIDS TO FACE (#**6**).

EXPERIMENT WITH OTHER EARS AND EYES.

12. STITCH HALVES OF MOUTH TO TOP AND BOTTOM SECTIONS OF HEAD (#**6**).

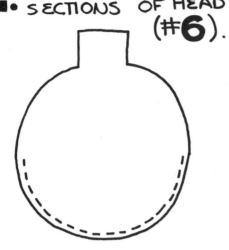 

13. STITCH THE SIDES OF THE HEAD TOGETHER.

14. STUFF HEAD BUT NOT NECK

15. INSERT NECK INTO BODY. PLACE IT FLAT AGAINST THE BAT'S BACK. PIN AND STITCH OPENING CLOSED BY HAND.

16. MACHINE STITCH WITH ZIPPER FOOT AROUND TOP OF WINGS.

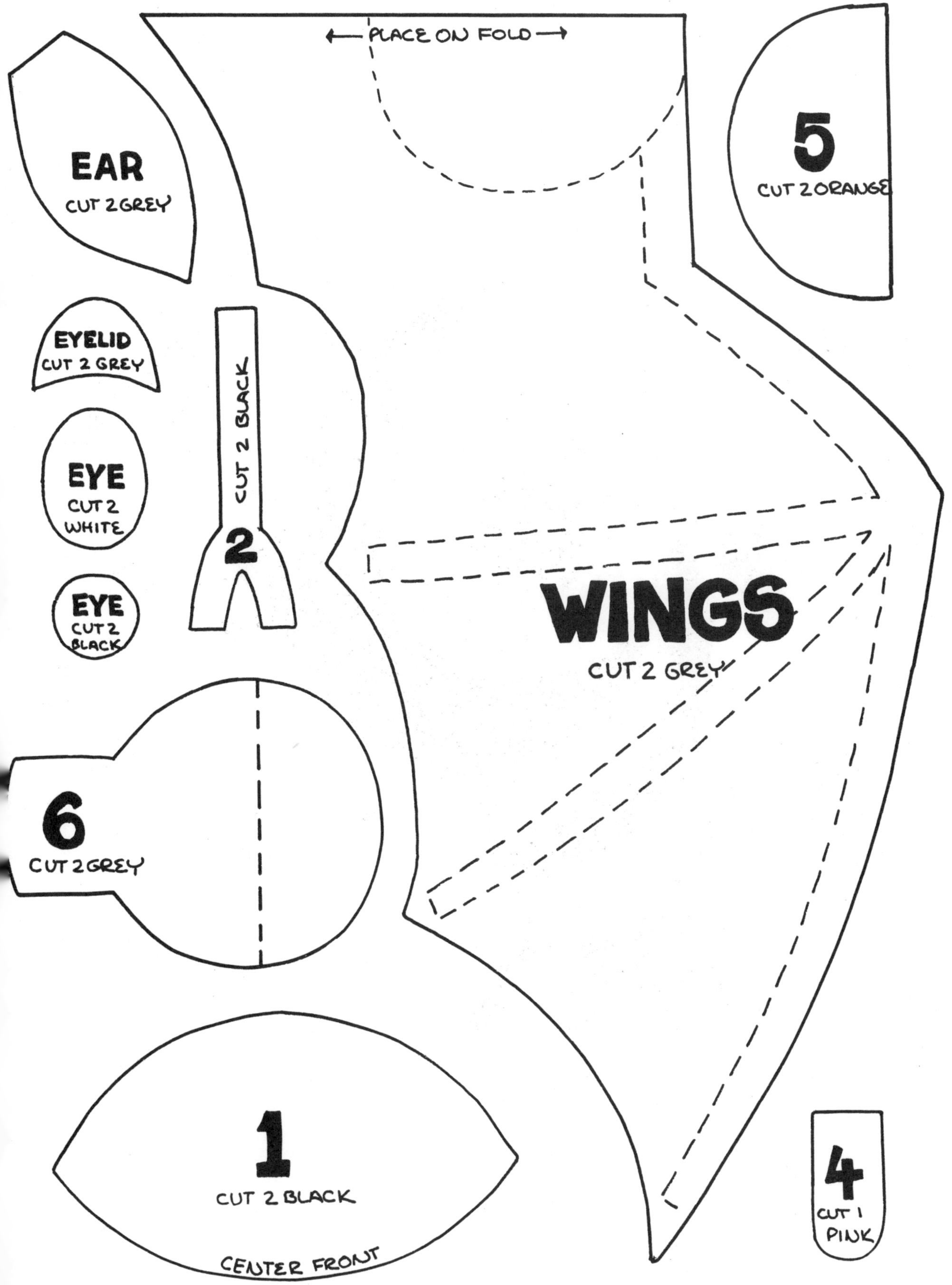

EAR
CUT 2 GREY

EYELID
CUT 2 GREY

EYE
CUT 2
WHITE

EYE
CUT 2
BLACK

2
CUT 2 BLACK

PLACE ON FOLD

5
CUT 2 ORANGE

WINGS
CUT 2 GREY

6
CUT 2 GREY

1
CUT 2 BLACK

CENTER FRONT

4
CUT 1
PINK

BEE

YOU WILL NEED:
POLYESTER FIBER FILL
30"x9½" BLACK FELT
18" x 9" WHITE FELT
9"x10" YELLOW FELT
ONE 6"BLACK PIPE
CLEANER

1. STITCH THE YELLOW STRIPES (A,B,C) ON PIECES #1. MAKE BOTH SIDES MATCH.

2. PLACE PIECES #3 ON PIECES #2. PLACE PIECES #4 ON PIECES #3. PLACE PIECES #5 ON PIECES #4. STITCH AROUND #5. DRAW LINES WITH A FELT TIP PEN ON #4.

3. STITCH AROUND NOSE (#6). STUFF. (PATIENCE AND KNITTING NEEDLE REQUIRED.)

4. BEND 6" PIPECLEANER OVER ¼" AT BOTH ENDS. BEND IN HALF.

5. INSERT NOSE AND ANTENNAE (PIPECLEANER) BETWEEN HALVES OF FACE. STITCH.

6. PIN AND STITCH FACE TO #7. LEAVE AN OPENING FOR STUFFING. STUFF. MACHINE STITCH OPENING CLOSED.

7. STITCH AROUND WINGS #8. STUFF.

8. PIN HALVES OF BODY TOGETHER. INSERT AND PIN WINGS. STITCH FROM **A** TO **B**.

9. STUFF VERY FULL. FOLD FELT AT OPENING. PIN AND STITCH CLOSED BY HAND.

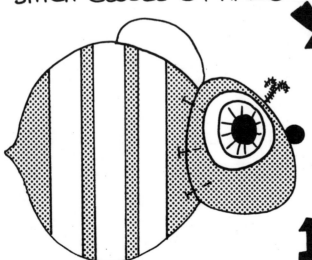

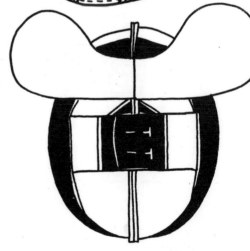

10. PIN HEAD TO BODY. HAND STITCH TOGETHER.

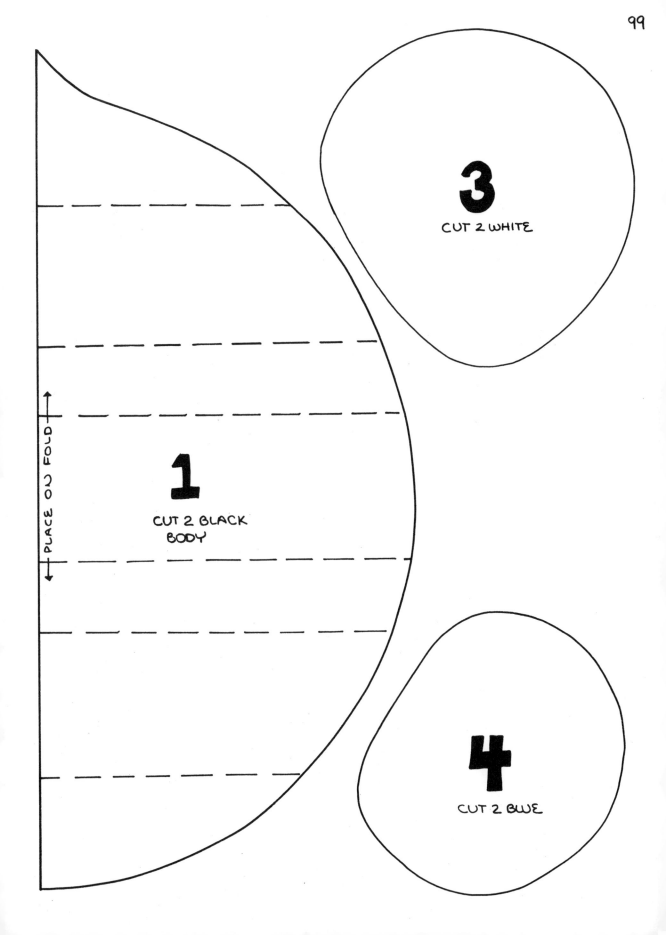

99

3

CUT 2 WHITE

PLACE ON FOLD

1

CUT 2 BLACK
BODY

4

CUT 2 BLUE

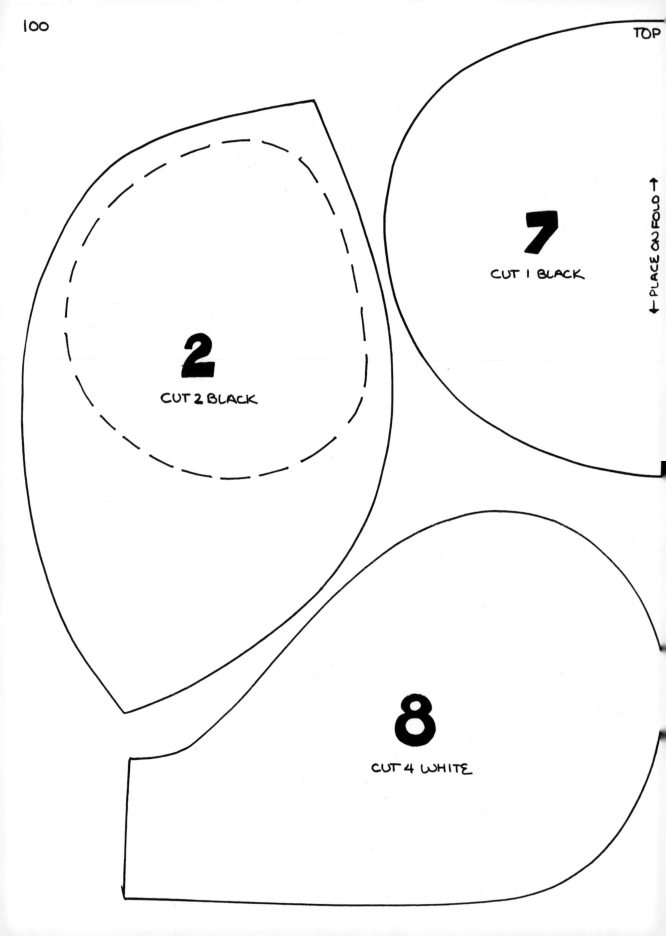

TOP

2

CUT 2 BLACK

7

CUT 1 BLACK

← PLACE ON FOLD →

8

CUT 4 WHITE

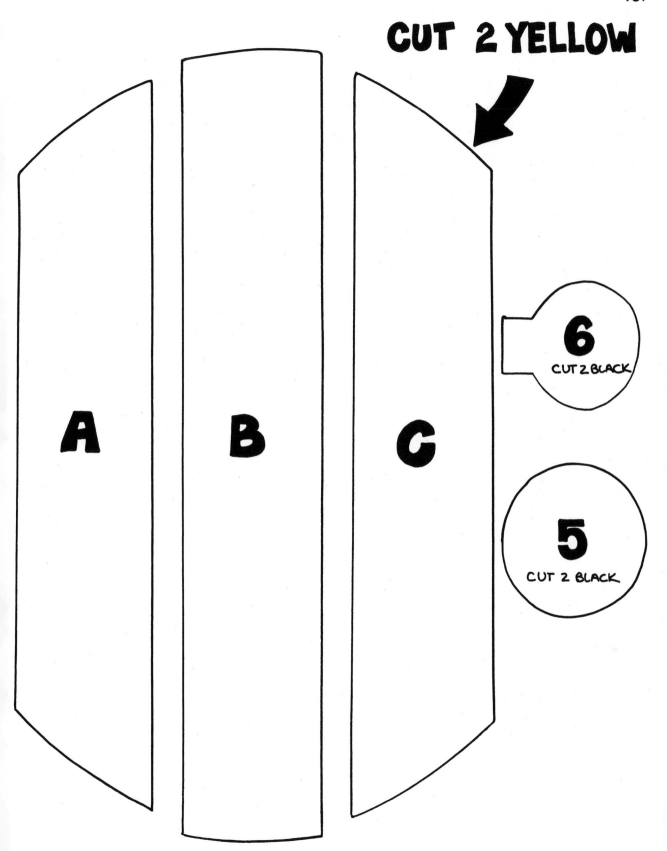

CUDDLEFLY

YOU WILL NEED:
   8" × 20" BLACK FELT
   14" × 39" YELLOW FELT
   9" × 26" ORANGE FELT
   6" × 20" PINK FELT
   SCRAPS OF WHITE AND BROWN
   POLYESTER FIBER FILL

TO SIMPLIFY CON-
STRUCTION OF THE
CUDDLEFLY, BELOW
ARE DIAGRAMS OF
THE UPPER AND
LOWER HALVES OF
BOTH WINGS.

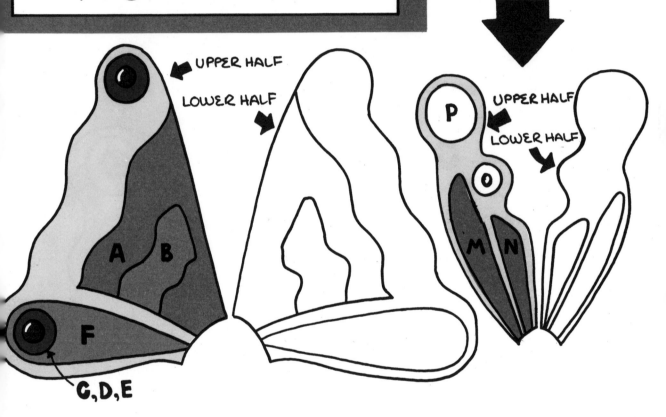

UPPER HALF

LOWER HALF

A B

F

G, D, E

UPPER HALF

LOWER HALF

P

O

M N

1. STITCH ALL DECORATIVE PIECES TO THE LOWER HALVES
OF THE LARGER WINGS AND BOTH HALVES OF THE SMALLER
WINGS.
(THE NEXT SIX STEPS WILL SHOW HOW TO DECORATE
THE UPPER HALF OF THE RIGHT UPPER WING. REPEAT
THE STEPS FOR THE LEFT UPPER WING.)

2. PLACE PIECE **A** ON WING. PLACE **B** ON TOP OF **A** AND STITCH AROUND PIECE **B** AS ILLUSTRATED.

3. STUFF **A** THROUGH OPENING, THEN STITCH FROM **X** TO **Y**.

4. PLACE PIECE **C** ON WING. PLACE **D** ON **C** AND **E** ON **D**. STITCH AROUND PIECE **E**.

5. PLACE ANOTHER **C** ON PIECE **F**. PLACE PIECES **D** AND **E** ON TOP OF THAT. STITCH AROUND **E**.

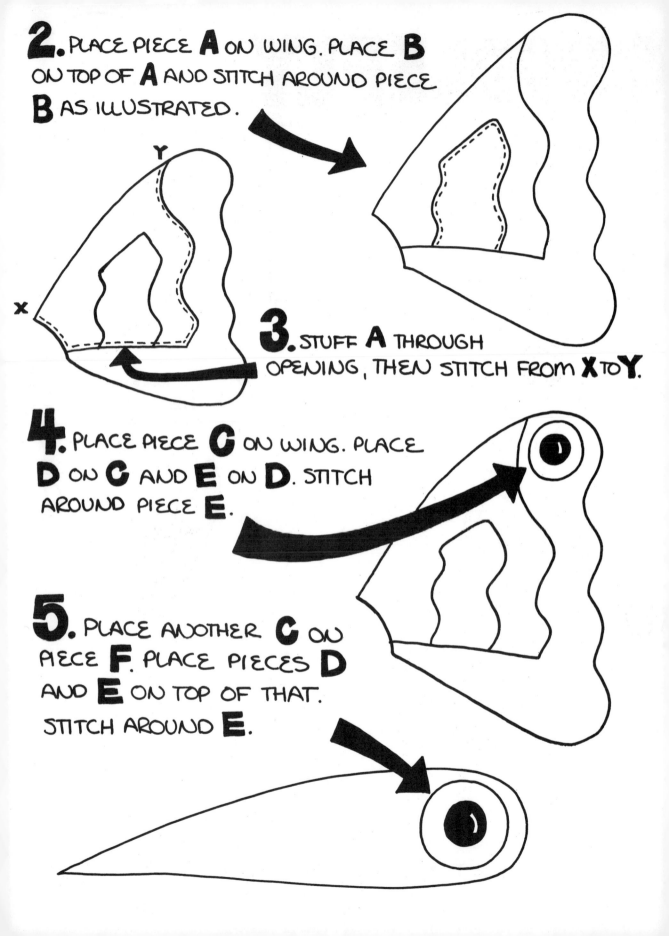

6. PLACE **F** ON THE WING AND STITCH.

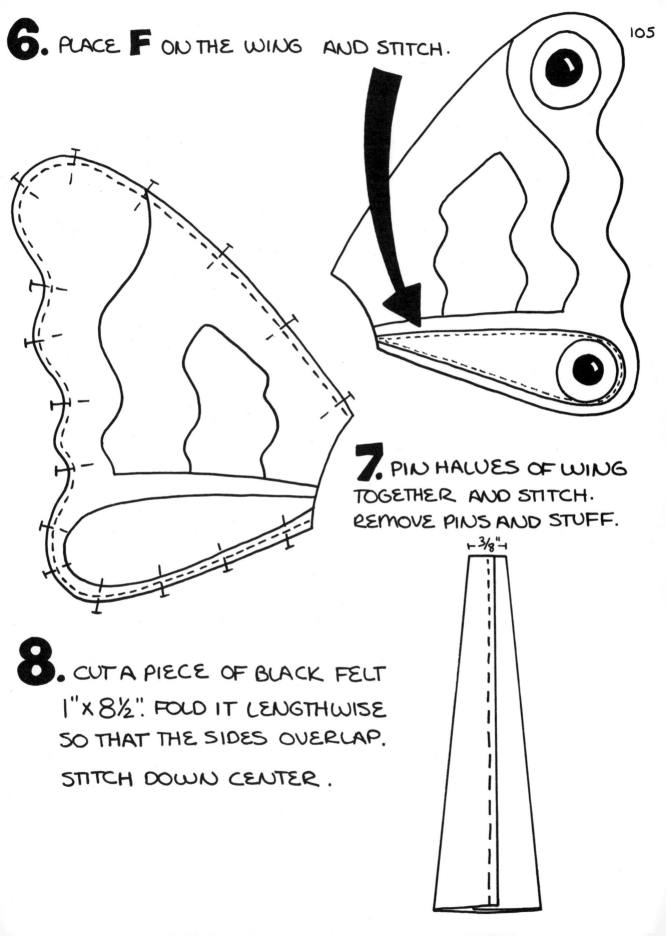

7. PIN HALVES OF WING TOGETHER AND STITCH. REMOVE PINS AND STUFF.

8. CUT A PIECE OF BLACK FELT 1" X 8½". FOLD IT LENGTHWISE SO THAT THE SIDES OVERLAP. STITCH DOWN CENTER.

3/8"

10. CUT THE STRIP IN HALF AND MACHINE TACK A PIECE **#3** TO EACH STRIP.

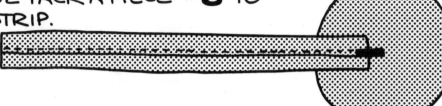

11. ATTACH EYES AND MOUTH TO FACE (**#4**).

12.

PIN ANTENNAE. BETWEEN FRONT AND BACK OF HEAD. STITCH AROUND HEAD.

13. STUFF.

14. STITCH HEAD TO PIECE #**5**.

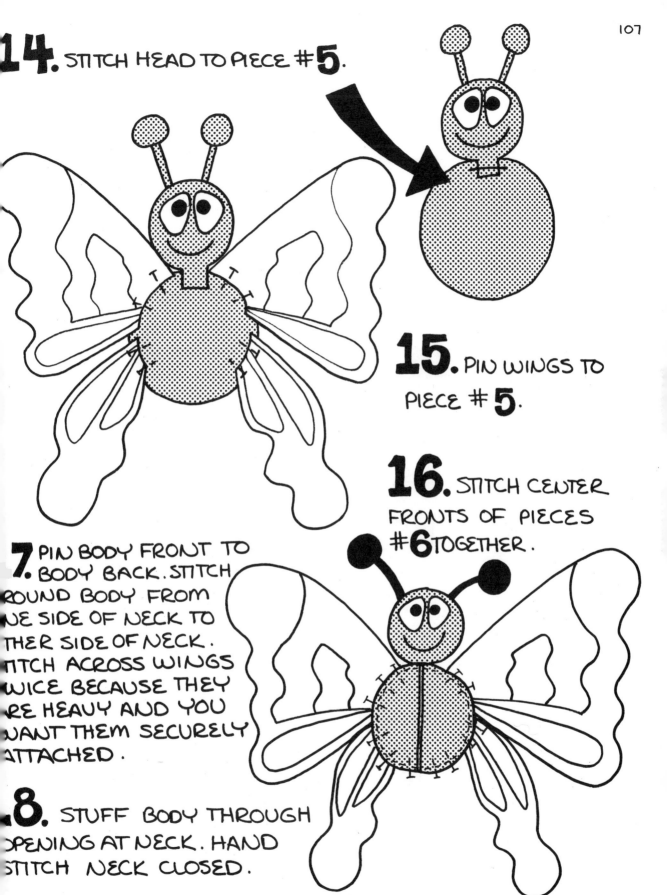

15. PIN WINGS TO PIECE #**5**.

16. STITCH CENTER FRONTS OF PIECES #**6** TOGETHER.

7. PIN BODY FRONT TO BODY BACK. STITCH ROUND BODY FROM NE SIDE OF NECK TO THER SIDE OF NECK. TITCH ACROSS WINGS WICE BECAUSE THEY RE HEAVY AND YOU WANT THEM SECURELY ATTACHED.

8. STUFF BODY THROUGH OPENING AT NECK. HAND STITCH NECK CLOSED.

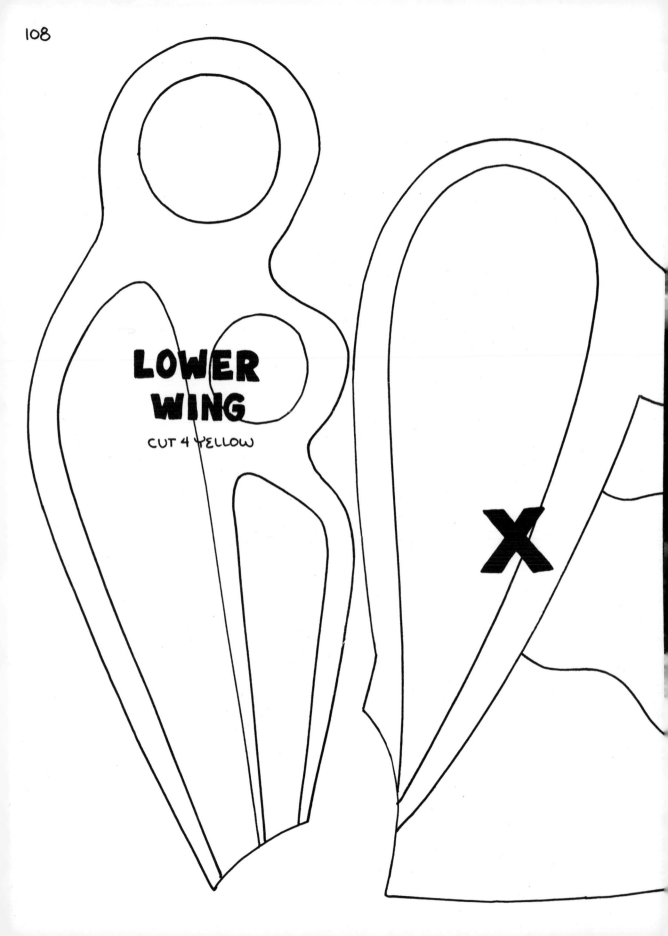

108

LOWER
WING

CUT 4 YELLOW

X

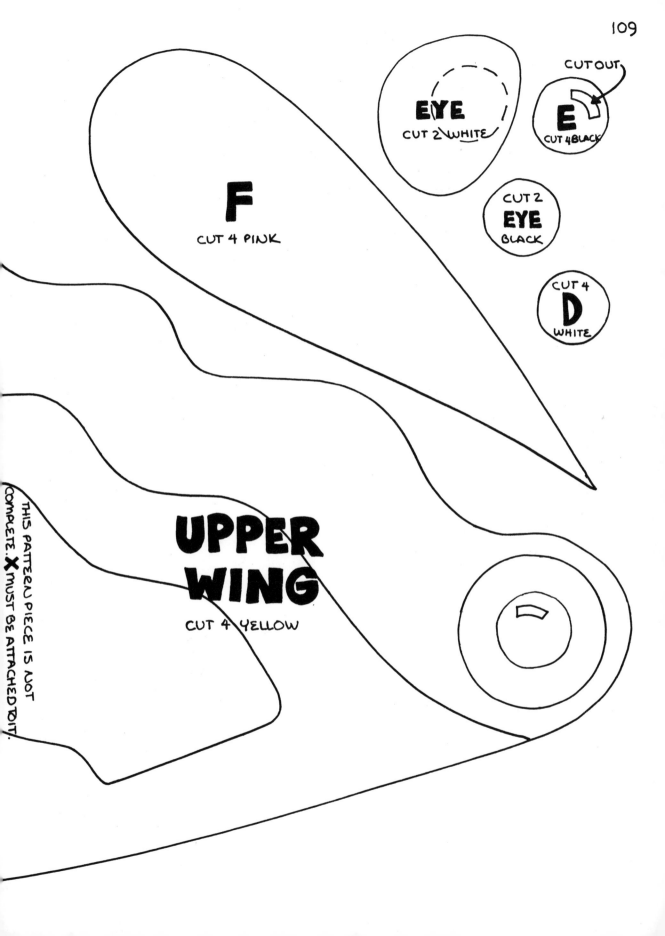

EYE
CUT 2 WHITE

CUTOUT

E
CUT 4 BLACK

F
CUT 4 PINK

CUT 2
EYE
BLACK

CUT 4
D
WHITE

UPPER
WING
CUT 4 YELLOW

THIS PATTERN PIECE IS NOT COMPLETE. **X** MUST BE ATTACHED TO IT.

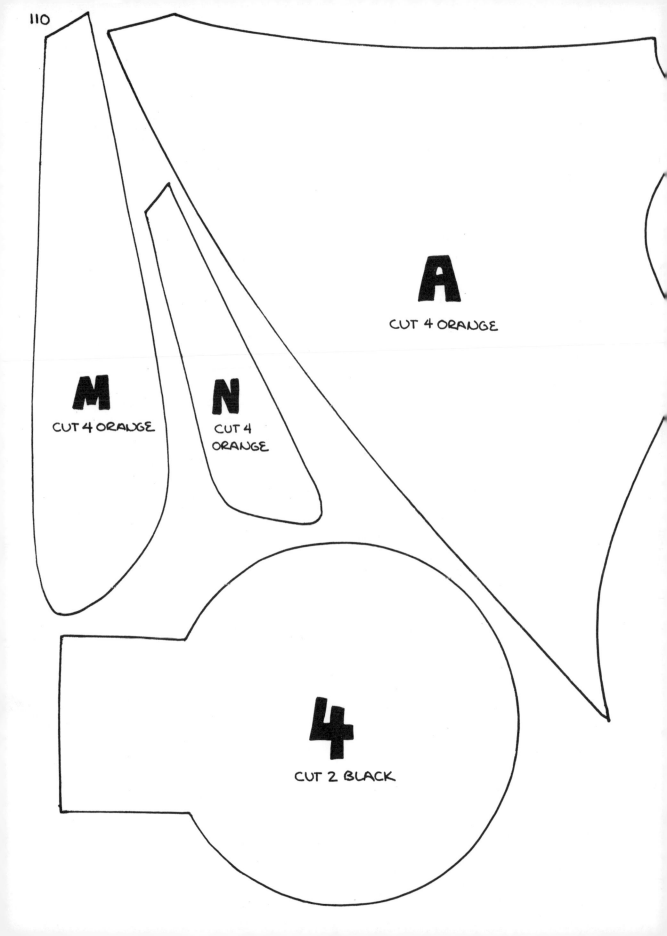

110

A

CUT 4 ORANGE

M

CUT 4 ORANGE

N

CUT 4
ORANGE

4

CUT 2 BLACK

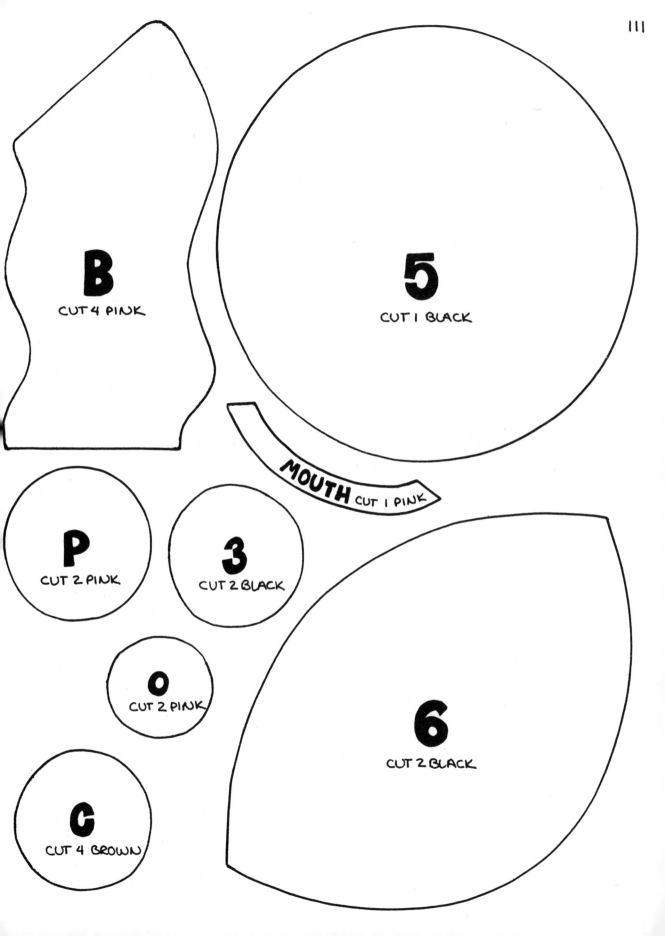

B
CUT 4 PINK

5
CUT 1 BLACK

MOUTH CUT 1 PINK

P
CUT 2 PINK

3
CUT 2 BLACK

0
CUT 2 PINK

6
CUT 2 BLACK

C
CUT 4 BROWN

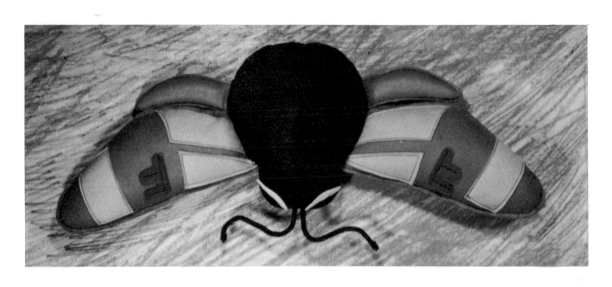

EUCHROMIA FORMOSA MOTH

YOU WILL NEED: ·
POLYESTER FIBER FILL
ONE 12" PIPE CLEANER
11"x17" BLACK FELT
10"x 36" BROWN FELT
SCRAPS OF GREEN,
WHITE, ORANGE, YELLOW,
TURQUOISE FELT

1. STITCH STRIPES OF COLOR (A,B,C,D,E) TO EUCHROMIA'S BACK (#**1**).

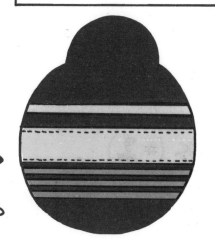

2. STITCH DECORATIVE PATTERNS (M,N,O,P,Q,R) ON WINGS.

LARGER WINGS (#**2**) HAVE SAME PATTERN ON BOTH SIDES.

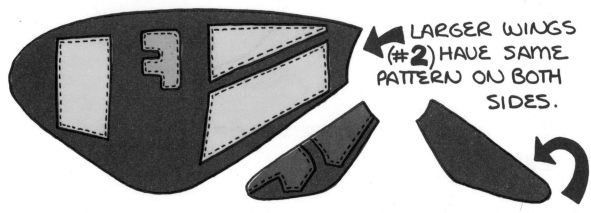

SMALLER WINGS (#**3**) HAVE NO PATTERN ON UNDERSIDE.

3. STITCH BOTH HALVES OF LARGER AND SMALLER WINGS TOGETHER. STUFF.

4. BEND 12" PIPE CLEANER INTO SHAPE OF ANTENNAE. BEND OVER ENDS ¼".

5. HAND TACK THE PIPE CLEANER ON INSIDE OF BACK (#**1**).

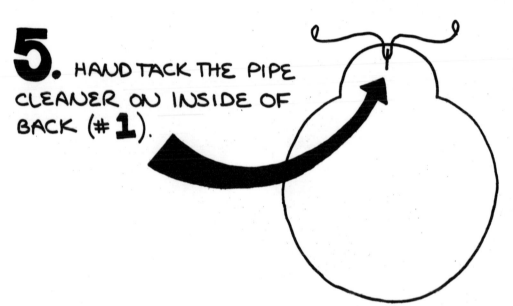

6. STITCH CENTER FRONTS OF PIECES #**4** TOGETHER.

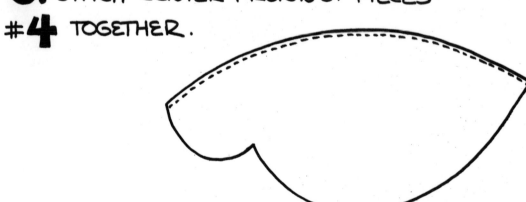

7. PIN WINGS TO BACK STARTING AT NECK NOTCH.

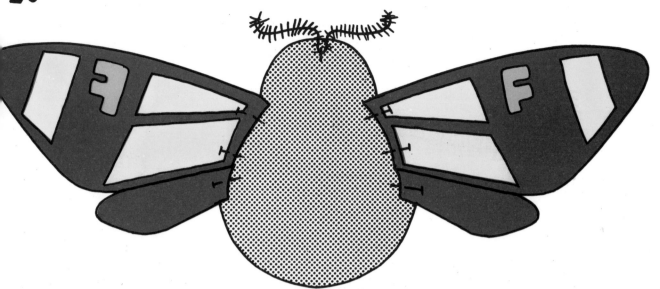

8. PIN FRONT TO BACK. STITCH AROUND BODY. LEAVE OPENING FOR STUFFING.

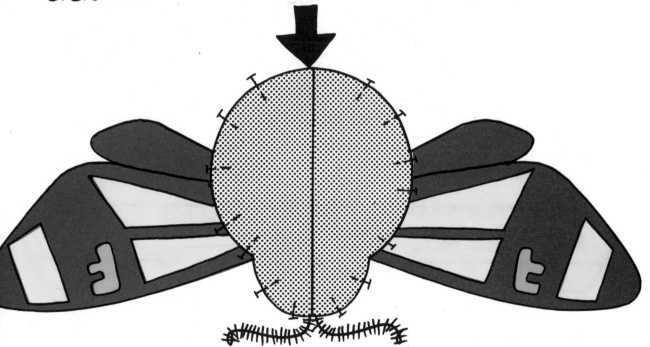

9. STUFF. MACHINE STITCH OPENING CLOSED.

10. STITCH EYES ON FACE BY HAND.

116

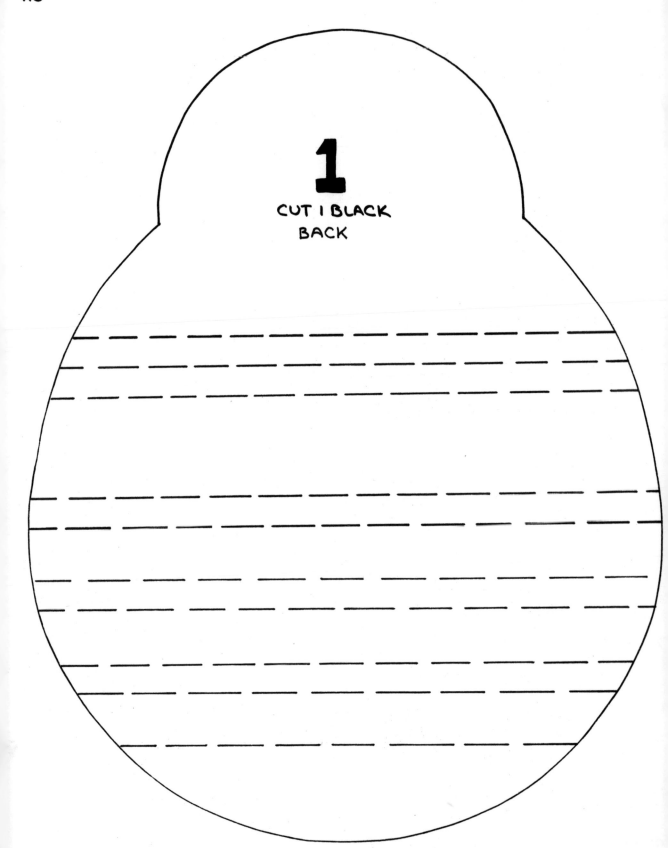

1

CUT 1 BLACK
BACK

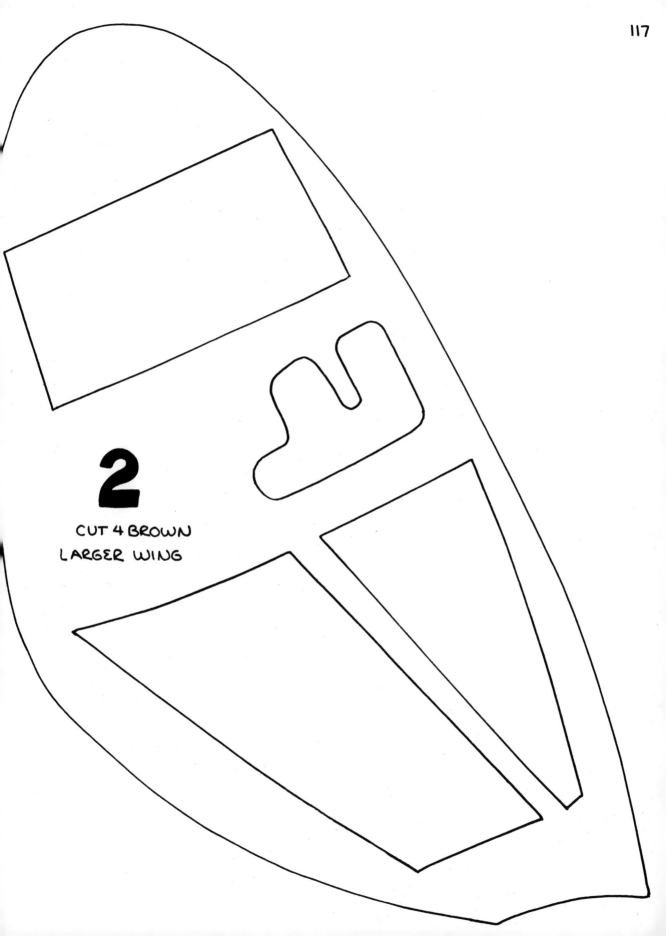

2

CUT 4 BROWN
LARGER WING

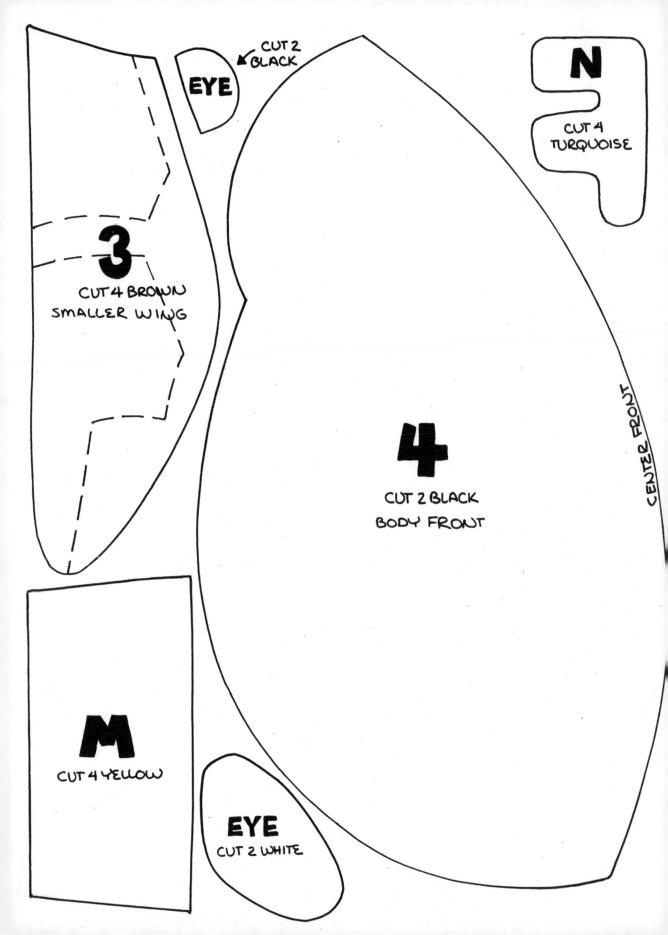

EYE
CUT 2 BLACK

N
CUT 4 TURQUOISE

3
CUT 4 BROWN
SMALLER WING

4
CUT 2 BLACK
BODY FRONT

CENTER FRONT

M
CUT 4 YELLOW

EYE
CUT 2 WHITE

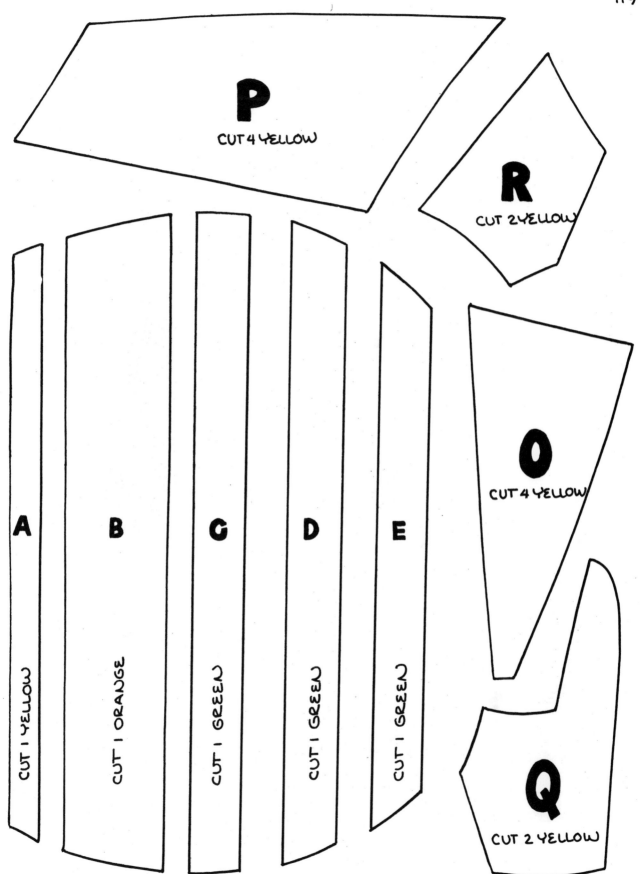

RED SEA BUTTERFLY FISH

YOU WILL NEED:
POLYESTER FIBER FILL
7"x28" BLUE FELT
22"x12" WHITE FELT
9"x11" ORANGE FELT
8"x12" BLACK FELT

1. PLACE PIECES #1 ON TOP OF PIECES #2. OVERLAP TO LINE INDICATED ON PATTERN PIECE #2. STITCH.

2. STITCH WHITE LINES (A,B,C,D,E,F,G) TO BLUE SIDES.

3. STITCH EYES (#7) TO FACE (#3).

4. PLACE BLUE SIDES WITH WHITE STRIPES OVER PIECES #3. OVERLAP TO LINE INDICATED ON PATTERN PIECE #3. PIN AND STITCH.

5. STITCH OR DRAW LINES ON #8. PIN PATTERN PIECES #4 OVER SEAM WHERE ORANGE AND BLUE MEET. INSERT FINS (#8). STITCH.

6. PLACE THE COMPLETED SECTIONS OVER PIECES #5. PLACE #6 PIECES OVER THAT. PIN AND STITCH.

7. STITCH THE TWO HALVES OF THE FISH TOGETHER. LEAVE OPENING FOR STUFFING. STUFF. MACHINE STITCH OPENING CLOSED. TRIM.

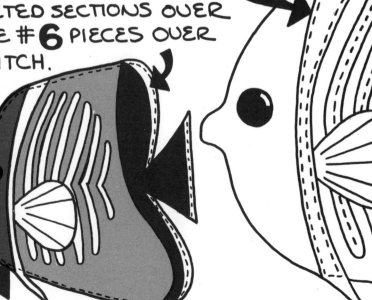

122

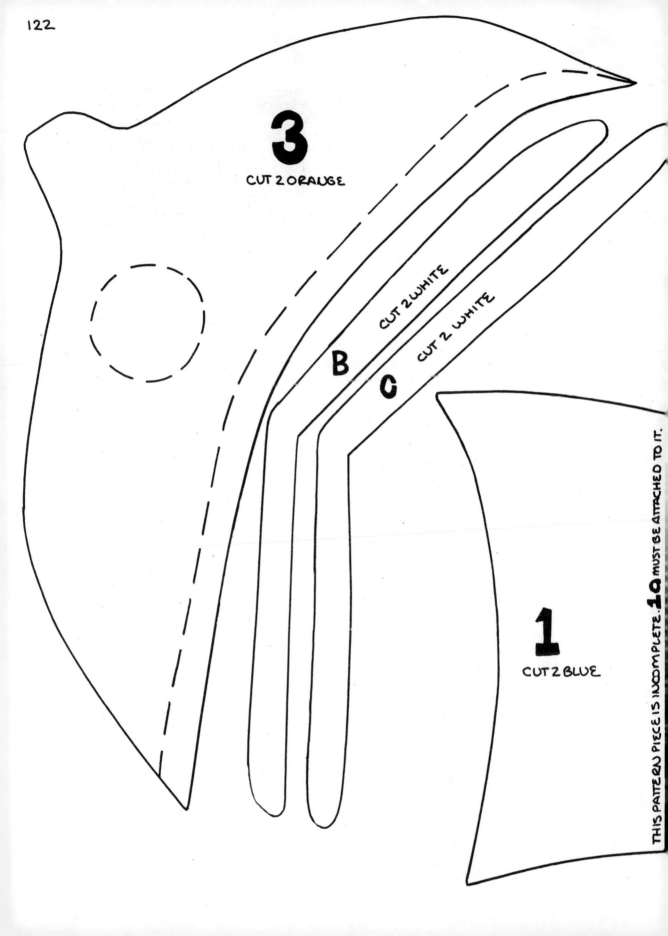

3

CUT 2 ORANGE

CUT 2 WHITE

CUT 2 WHITE

B

C

1

CUT 2 BLUE

THIS PATTERN PIECE IS INCOMPLETE. **1a** MUST BE ATTACHED TO IT.

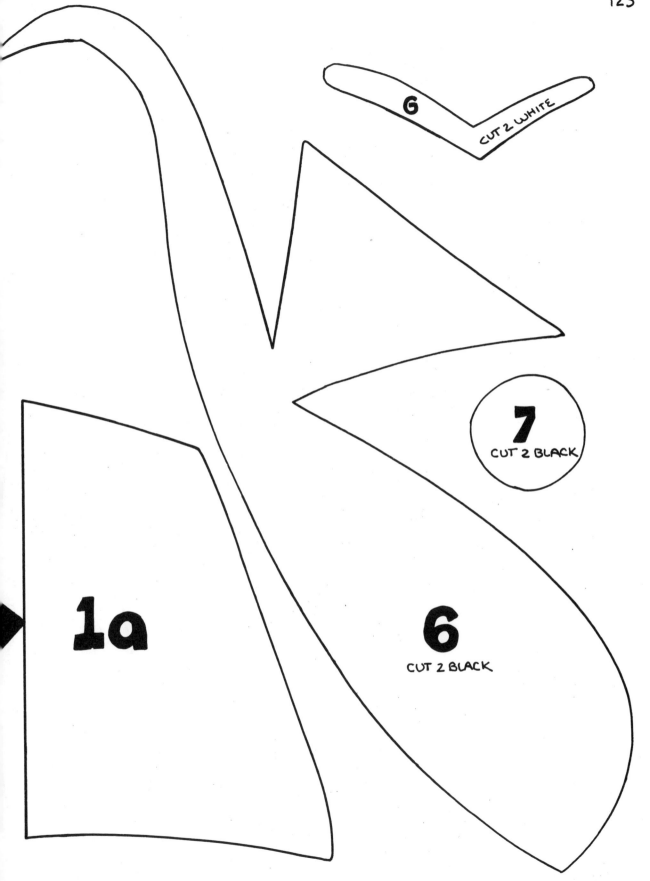

6

CUT 2 WHITE

7

CUT 2 BLACK

1a

6

CUT 2 BLACK

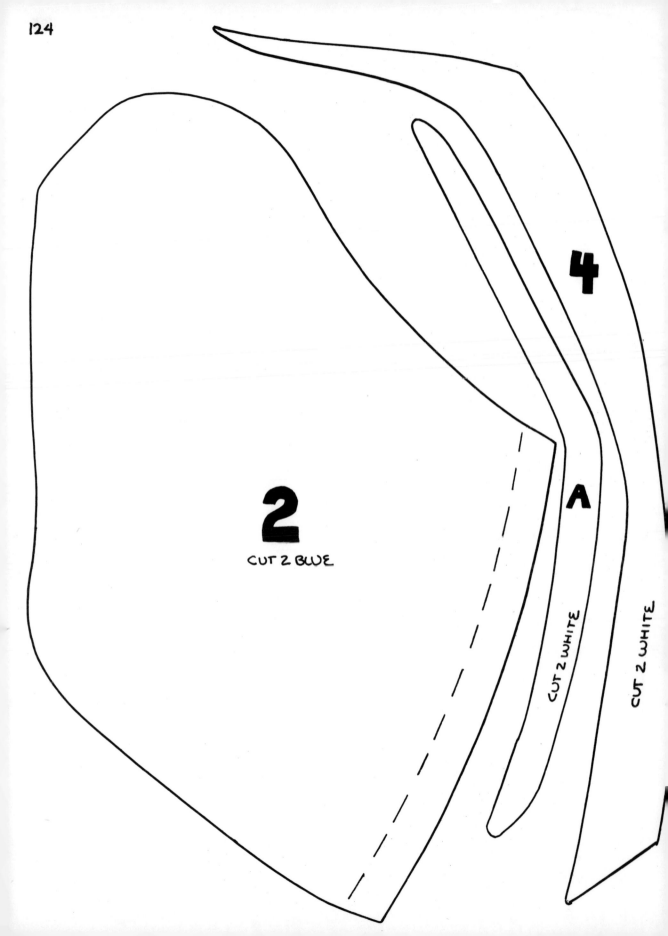

2

CUT 2 BLUE

A

4

CUT 2 WHITE

CUT 2 WHITE

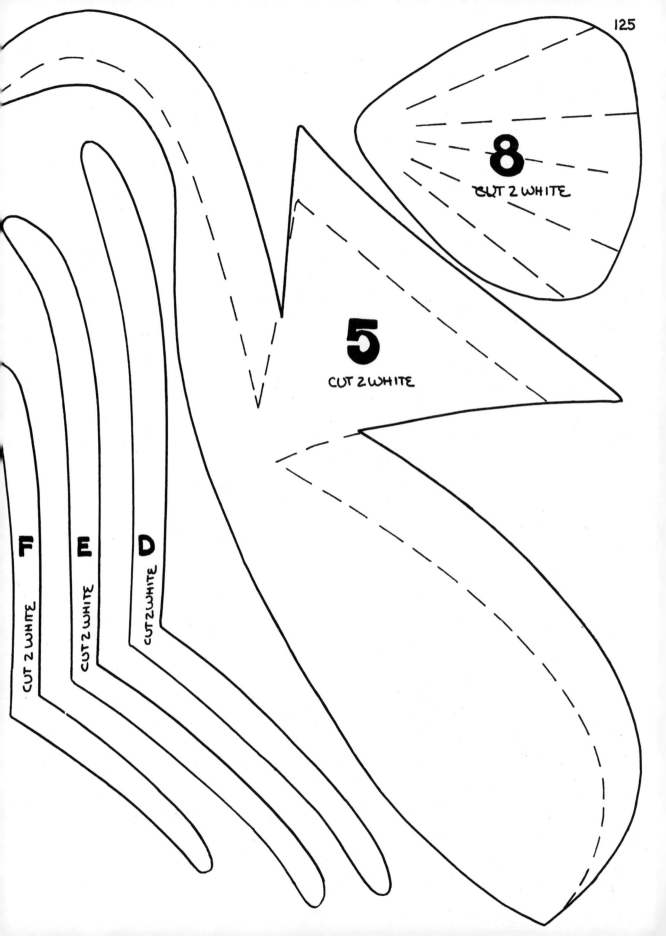

125

8
CUT 2 WHITE

5
CUT 2 WHITE

F
CUT 2 WHITE

E
CUT 2 WHITE

D
CUT 2 WHITE

RACCOON

YOU WILL NEED:
POLYESTER FIBER FILL
24" × 10" WHITE FELT
29" × 9" BROWN FELT
14" × 10" BLACK FELT
BLUE FELT SCRAPS

1. STITCH BLACK MASK TO BOTH SIDES OF FACE (#**1**).

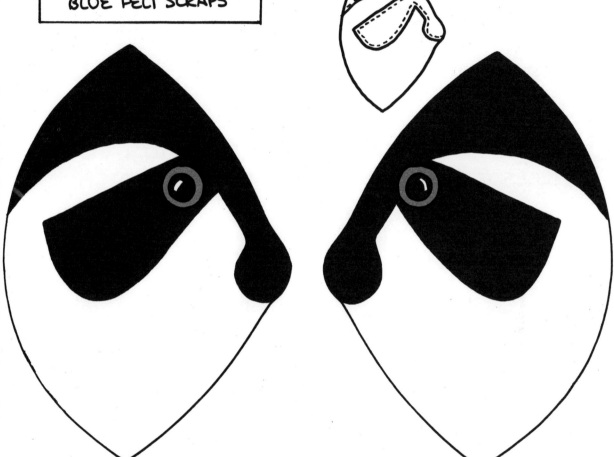

2. STITCH EYES TO FACE. PLACE #**4** ON #**3** ON #**2**. POSITION ON FACE AND STITCH AROUND #**4**.

3. STITCH THE TWO HALVES OF THE FACE TOGETHER.

4. STITCH BLACK PIECES #**5** TO WHITE PIECES #**6**. PLACE THESE ON BROWN PIECES #**6** AND STITCH AROUND, THUS FORMING THE EARS.

5. STUFF THE EARS VERY LOOSELY.

6. PIN EARS TO PIECE #**7**. (POSITION INDICATED ON PATTERN.) PIN FACE TO #**7**. STITCH AROUND LEAVING OPENING FOR STUFFING.

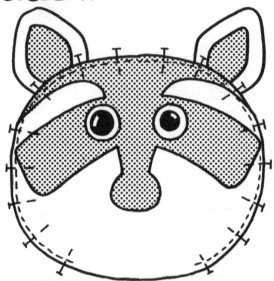

7. STUFF. STITCH OPENING CLOSED.

8. STITCH BLACK STRIPES (**A,B,C,D**) TO TAIL PIECES (#**8**). MAKE SURE BOTH SIDES MATCH.

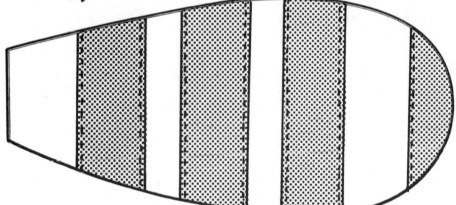

9. STITCH HALVES OF TAIL TOGETHER.

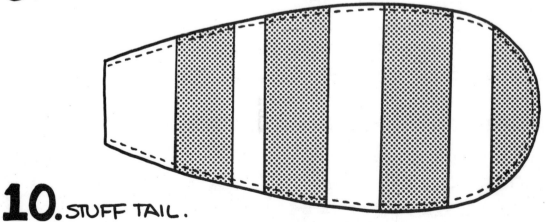

10. STUFF TAIL.

11.

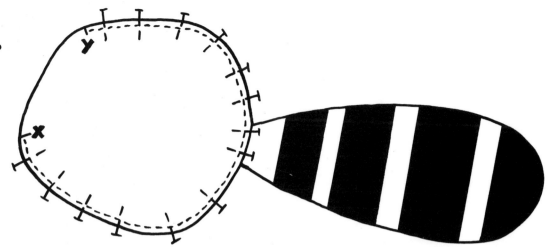

PIN TAIL BETWEEN HALVES OF BODY. STITCH FROM **X** TO **Y**. (INDICATED ON PATTERN PIECE #**9**.)

12. STUFF BODY.

13. FOLD THE FELT AT THE OPENING. PIN AND STITCH CLOSED BY HAND OR BY MACHINE.

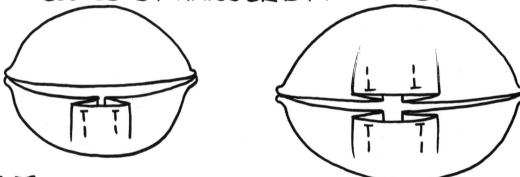

14. PIN THE HEAD TO THE BODY. STITCH TOGETHER BY HAND.

15. STITCH THE TWO FORELEGS AND THE TWO HIND LEGS TOGETHER. LEAVE OPENING FOR STUFFING. STUFF. MACHINE STITCH OPENING CLOSED. HAND STITCH LEGS TO BODY. POSITIONS INDICATED ON PATTERN PIECE #**9**.

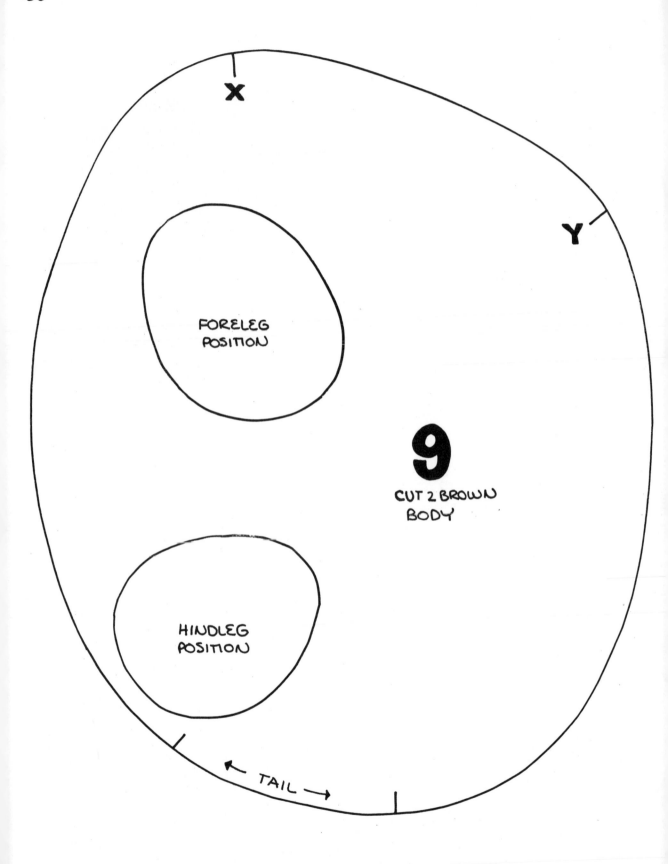

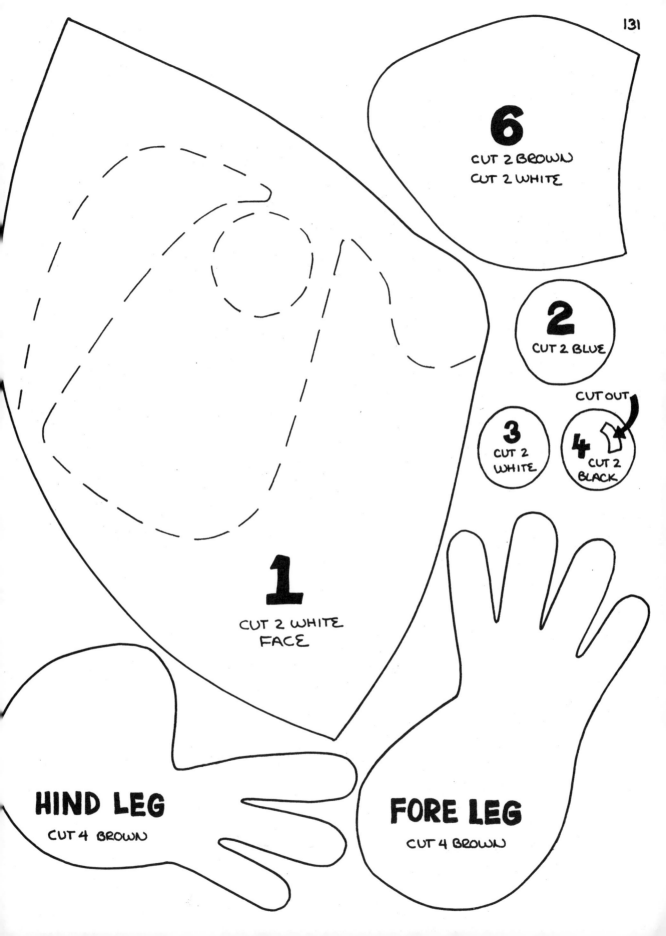

131

6

CUT 2 BROWN
CUT 2 WHITE

2

CUT 2 BLUE

CUT OUT

3

CUT 2
WHITE

4

CUT 2
BLACK

1

CUT 2 WHITE
FACE

HIND LEG

CUT 4 BROWN

FORE LEG

CUT 4 BROWN

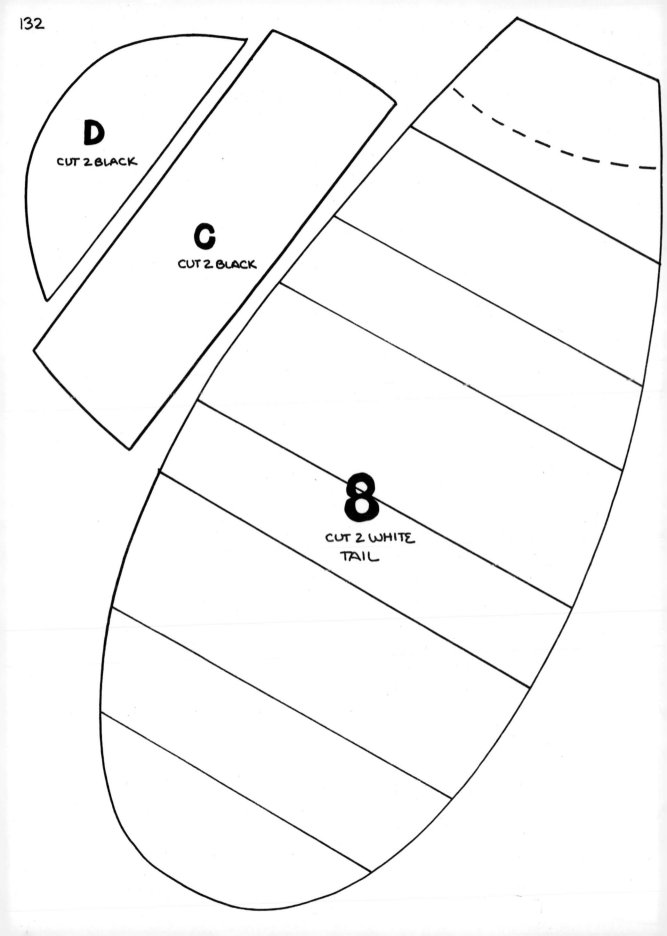

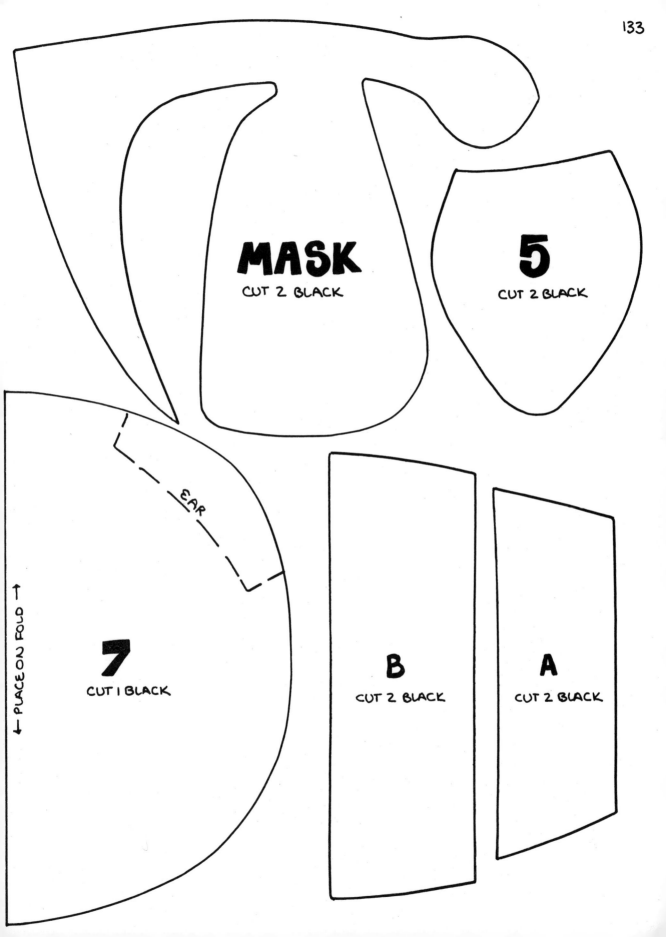

MASK
CUT 2 BLACK

5
CUT 2 BLACK

EAR

← PLACE ON FOLD →

7
CUT 1 BLACK

B
CUT 2 BLACK

A
CUT 2 BLACK

PUFFIN MASK

YOU WILL NEED:
WHITE POSTER BOARD
BLACK INK
RED/GREY MARKERS
STRING
ORANGE, WHITE, BLACK
AND YELLOW-ORANGE
FELT SCRAPS

THIS MASK IS DESIGNED FOR EYES THAT ARE 2½" PUPIL TO PUPIL. MEASURE THE DISTANCE BETWEEN YOUR EYES AND ADJUST THE PUFFIN'S EYES CLOSER TOGETHER OR FURTHER APART.

1. CUT RIGHT AND LEFT FACE OUT OF WHITE POSTER BOARD.

2. TRANSFER FACIAL FEATURES TO POSTER BOARD. INK IN BLACK AREAS AND COLOR EYES. CUT OUT EYE HOLES.

3. CUT OUT FELT PIECES.

4. PLACE WHITE PIECE #1 OVER BLACK PIECE #2 ON ORANGE BILL #3. STITCH ALONG BOTH SIDES OF WHITE PIECE. REPEAT FOR OTHER HALF OF BILL.

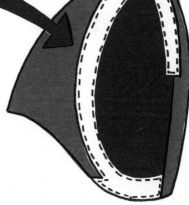

5. PLACE LEFT BILL ON LEFT FACE. STITCH FROM A TO B. DO SAME FOR RIGHT.

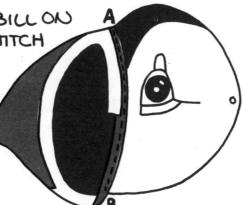

6. PLACE YELLOW ORANGE FLAP (#4) ON BILL AND ATTACH BY STITCHING MACHINE BACK AND FORTH.

7. PLACE WRONG SIDES TOGETHER AND STITCH BILL AROUND OUTSIDE EDGE.

8. PUNCH HOLES FOR STRING. ATTACH STRING.

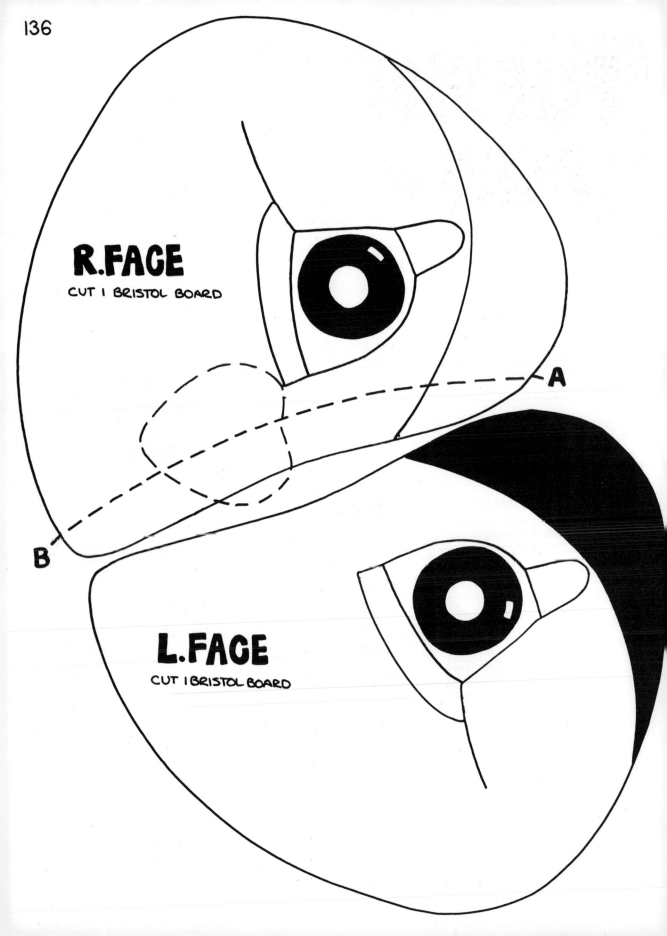

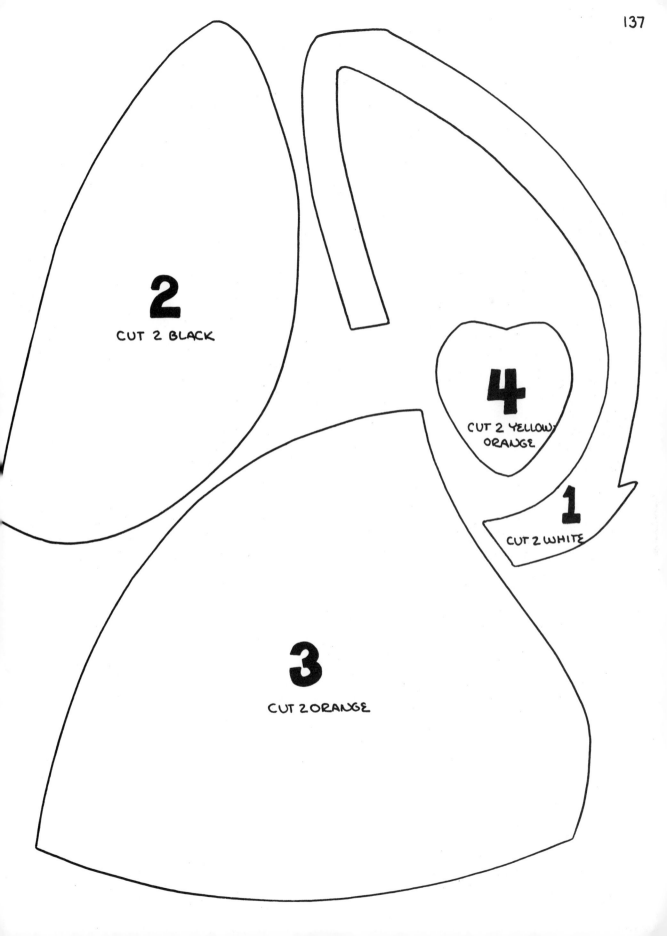

2

CUT 2 BLACK

4

CUT 2 YELLOW
ORANGE

1

CUT 2 WHITE

3

CUT 2 ORANGE

PIG MASK

YOU WILL NEED:
26" OF ¼" BLACK TAPE
14" x 36" PINK FELT
SCRAPS OF LIGHT PINK
  AND BLACK FELT
¼" x 3" FAKE FUR
POLYESTER FIBER FILL
18" OF 20 GAUGE WIRE

1. STITCH NOSTRILS (#**1**) TO SNOUT END (#**2**).

2. STITCH EYES TO #**7**. FLIP MASK OVER AND CUT AWAY PINK FELT ¼" FROM STITCHING LINE.

3. STITCH LIGHT PINK INNER EARS (#**4**) TO OUTER EARS (#**5**).

4. STITCH #**4**/#**5** COMBINATIONS TO THE REMAINING #**5**s.

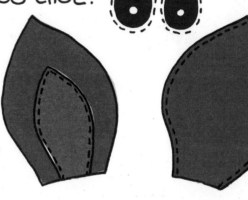

5.

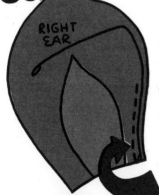

RIGHT EAR

CUT 18" WIRE IN HALF. TURN OVER ENDS ¼" THEN SHAPE ALONG INNER EDGES OF EARS. BEND ACROSS AT TOP. INSERT IN EAR. STITCH 3" WITH ZIPPER FOOT TO SECURE WIRE IN EAR.

6.

STITCH SNOUT (#**6**) TO SNOUT END (#**2**). STARTING ¼" FROM END OF #**6**, STITCH #**6** TO #**2** BY SLOWLY TURNING THE CIRCLE. ¼" OF 6 SHOULD BE LEFT OVER AT THE OTHER END.

7. STITCH  DOWN SNOUT. TRIM.

8. PIN AND BASTE SNOUT TO FACE (#**7**) WITH SEAM AT BOTTOM. LEAVE AN OPENING FOR STUFFING. STUFF. STITCH OPENING CLOSED.

9. STITCH FOREHEAD SEAM CLOSED.

10. CUT ¼"x3" FAKE FUR IN HALF. STITCH RIGHT SIDE OF FUR TO WRONG SIDE OF EYELID (#**8**). STITCH EYELIDS TO FACE.

11. FOLD EARS TO FIT BETWEEN **A** AND **B**. PIN TO MASK.

12. CUT 26" BLACK TAPE IN HALF AND PIN.

13. PIN FACING (#**9**) OVER EARS AND TIES AND STITCH. BE CAREFUL NOT TO BREAK YOUR SEWING MACHINE NEEDLE ON THE WIRES.

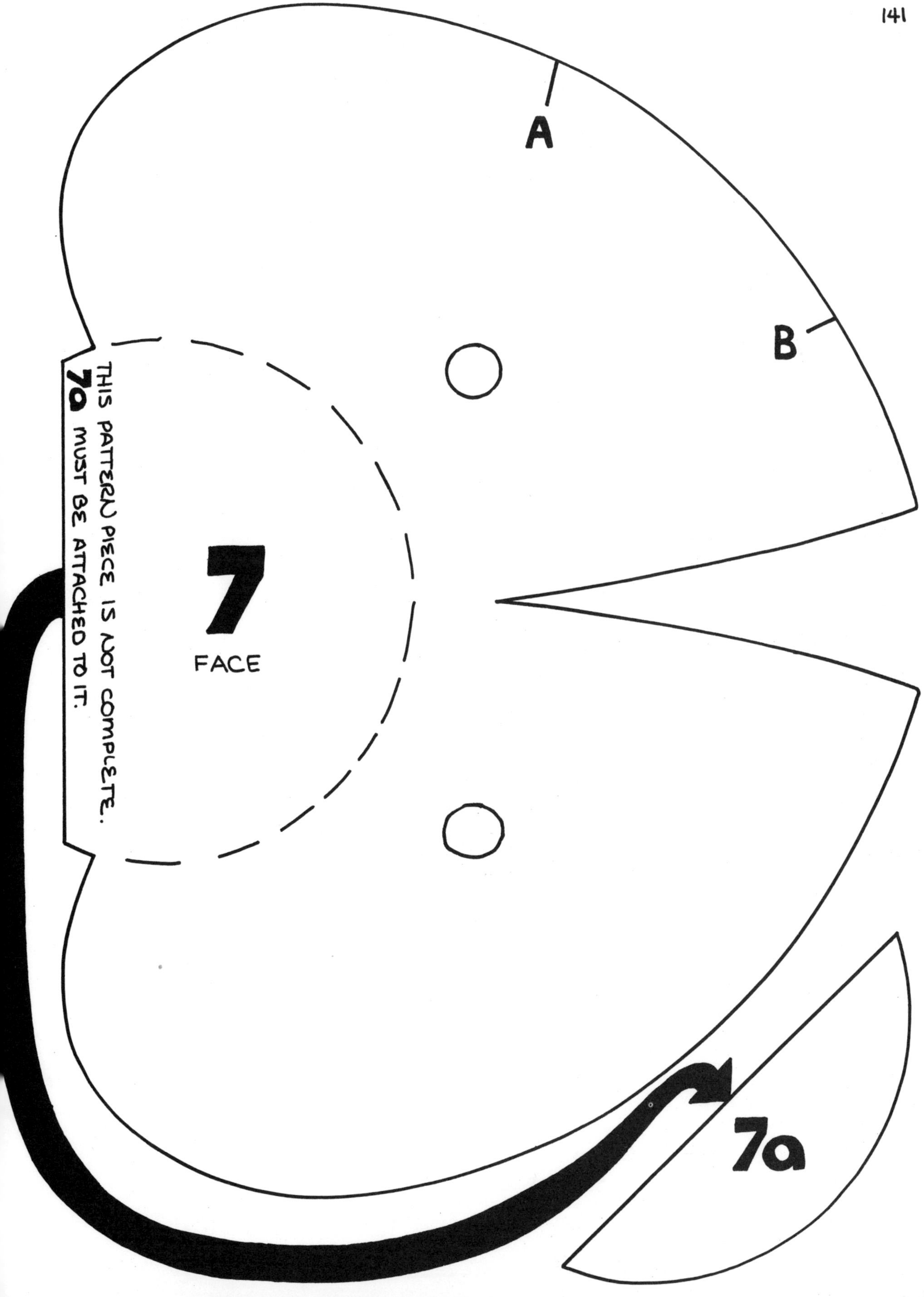

A

B

THIS PATTERN PIECE IS NOT COMPLETE.
7a MUST BE ATTACHED TO IT.

7a

7
FACE

7a

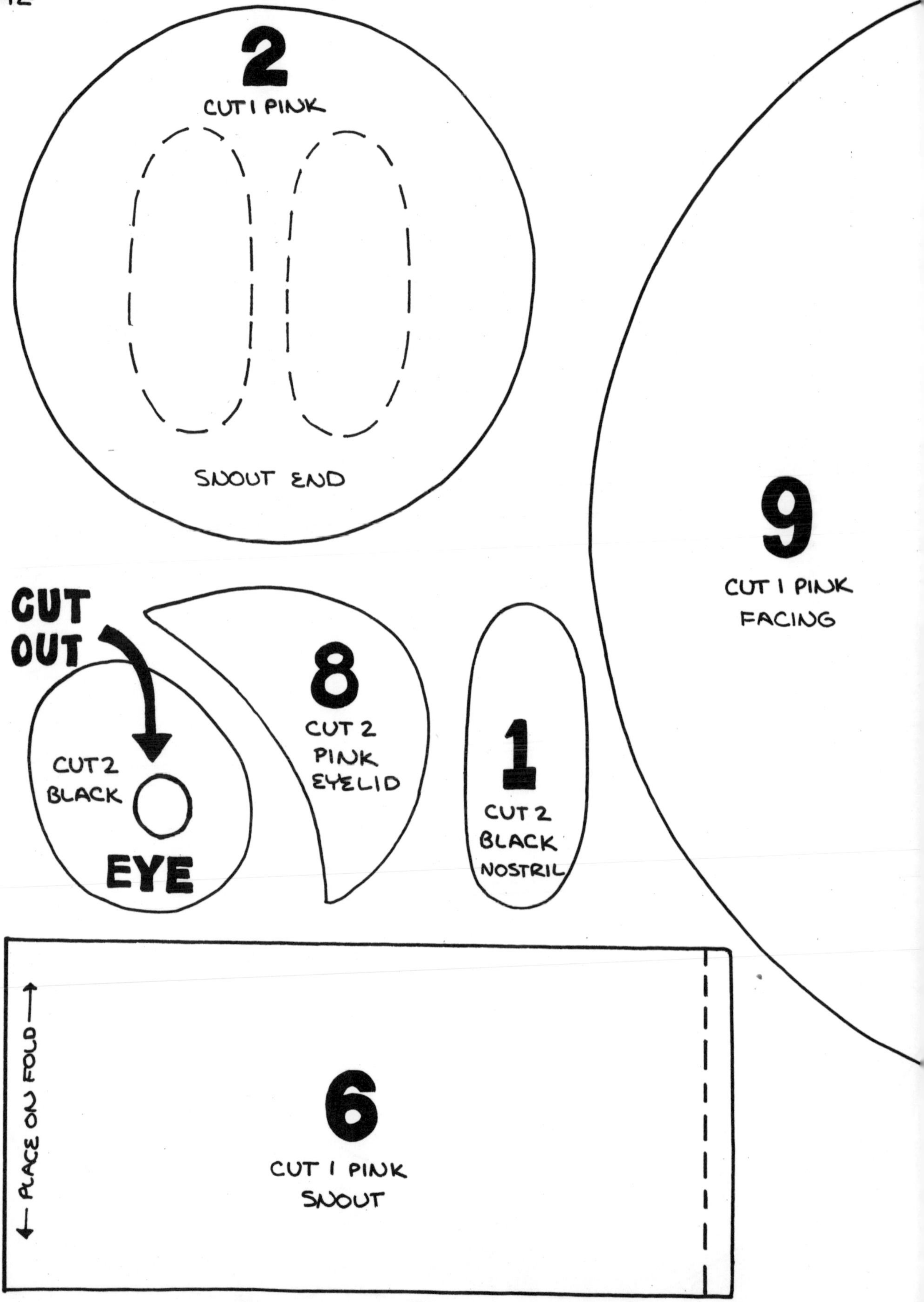

2

CUT 1 PINK

SNOUT END

9

CUT 1 PINK
FACING

CUT
OUT

8

CUT 2
PINK
EYELID

1

CUT 2
BLACK
NOSTRIL

CUT 2
BLACK

EYE

← PLACE ON FOLD →

6

CUT 1 PINK
SNOUT

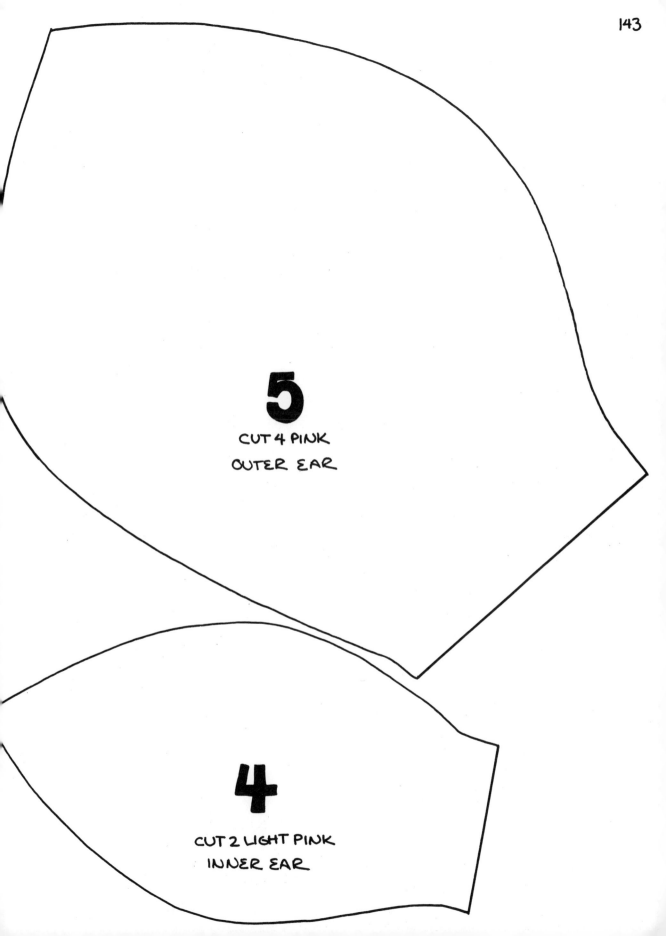

5

CUT 4 PINK

OUTER EAR

4

CUT 2 LIGHT PINK

INNER EAR

RAT MASK

YOU WILL NEED:
POLYESTER FIBER FILL
6-6" BLACK PIPE CLEANERS
5" x 36" GREY FELT
ORANGE, BLACK FELT SCRAPS
28" OF ¼" BLACK TAPE

1. PLACE PIECES **#1** ON PIECES **#2** ON PIECES **#3**. STITCH AROUND **#1** AND **#2**, THUS CREATING THE EARS.

2. INSERT NOSE BETWEEN RIGHT SIDES OF SNOUT (**#5**). STITCH. TURN RIGHT SIDE OUT.

3. STITCH RIGHT SIDE OF FOREHEAD (**#6**) TO RIGHT SIDE OF SNOUT.

4. STITCH EYES (**#7**) TO FACE. FLIP FACE OVER AND CUT AWAY GREY FELT ¼" FROM STITCHING LINE.

5. TO MAKE WHISKERS, LOOP ONE END OF EACH PIPE CLEANER ½".

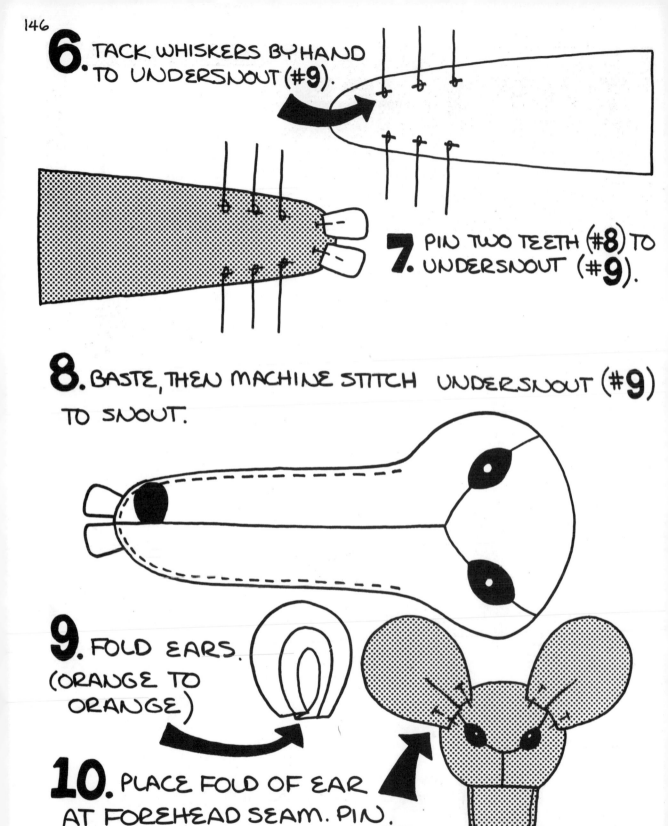

6. TACK WHISKERS BY HAND TO UNDERSNOUT (#**9**).

7. PIN TWO TEETH (#**8**) TO UNDERSNOUT (#**9**).

8. BASTE, THEN MACHINE STITCH UNDERSNOUT (#**9**) TO SNOUT.

9. FOLD EARS. (ORANGE TO ORANGE)

10. PLACE FOLD OF EAR AT FOREHEAD SEAM. PIN.

11. CUT 28" PIECE OF TAPE IN HALF AND PIN.

12. PIN AND BASTE FACING (#**10**) OVER EARS TO BACK OF FOREHEAD. STITCH.

13. STUFF SNOUT.

14. TACK TRAP (#**11**) AT SNOUT SEAM AND Y OF FOREHEAD.

15. WRINKLE SNOUT WITH HAND STITCHING. ALTERNATELY SECURE THREAD AND GATHER CENTER SNOUT SEAM.

16. DRAW WHISKER DOTS ON SNOUT WITH FELT TIP MARKER.

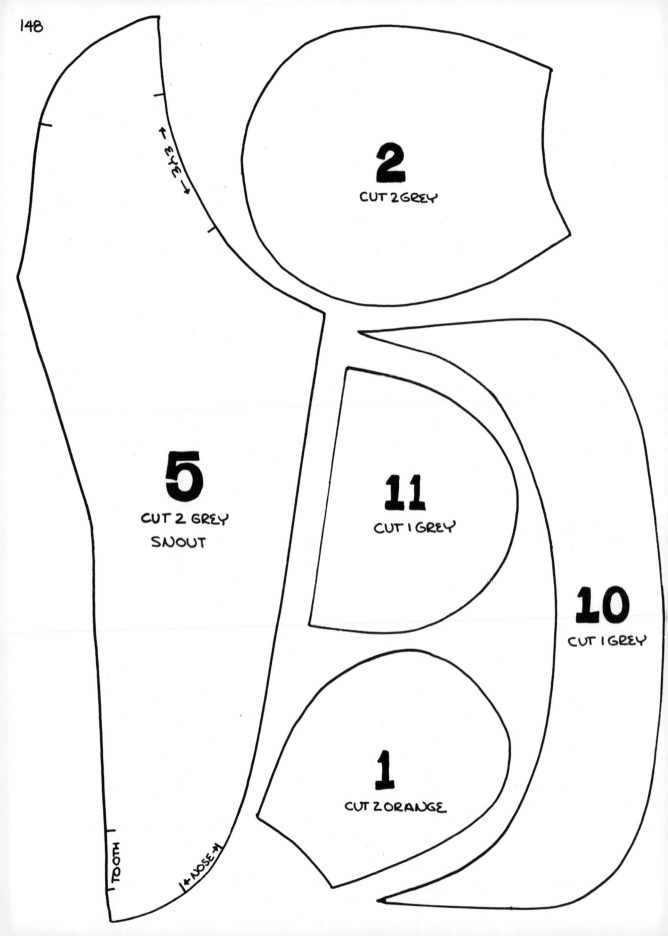

148

2
CUT 2 GREY

5
CUT 2 GREY
SNOUT

11
CUT I GREY

10
CUT I GREY

1
CUT 2 ORANGE

← EYE →

TOOTH

← NOSE →

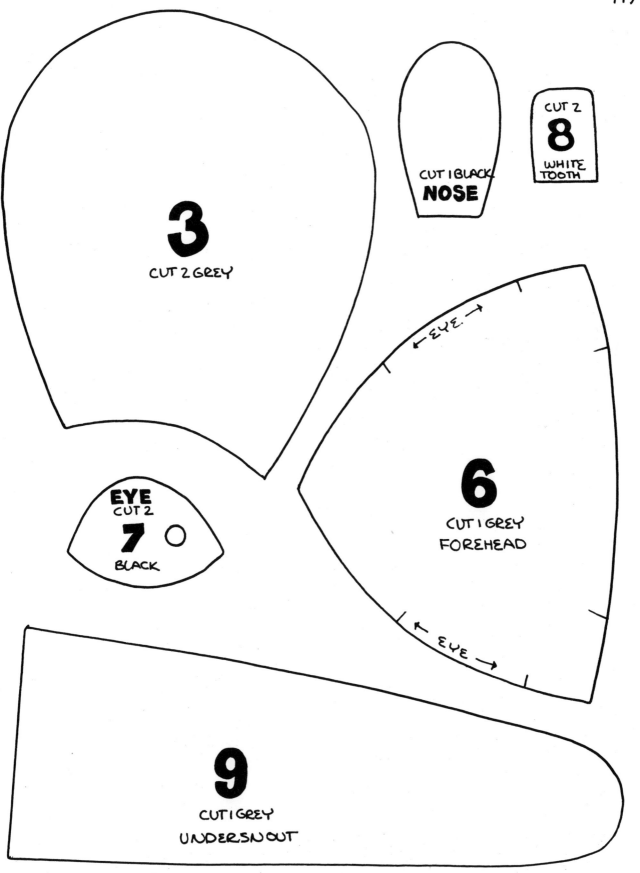

3
CUT 2 GREY

CUT 1 BLACK
NOSE

CUT 2
8
WHITE
TOOTH

←EYE→

6
CUT 1 GREY
FOREHEAD

← EYE →

EYE
CUT 2
7 ○
BLACK

9
CUT 1 GREY
UNDERSNOUT

FLAMINGO MASK

"one size fits all"

YOU WILL NEED:
POLYESTER FIBER FILL
9"x12" PIECE BRISTOL BOARD
(AVAILABLE IN ANY ART STORE)
SPRAY ADHESIVE
STRING
5"x18" BLACK FELT
12"x 8" WHITE FELT
8"x10" PINK FELT

1. PIN PIECE #**1** TO PIECE #**2**. PIN FROM CENTER OUT TO SIDES. STRETCH THE WHITE FELT THROUGH THE CURVE. STITCH.

START IN MIDDLE OVER-LAPPING 3/8".

2. NESTLE THE PINK BILL SECTION (#**3**) IN NEXT TO THE BLACK AND STITCH.

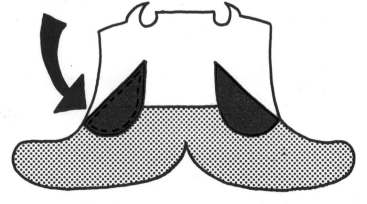

3. STITCH AROUND END OF BILL TO PINK PATCH

4. SPRAY THE BACK OF THE FELT FLAMINGO FACE (#**4**) WITH ADHESIVE AND CAREFULLY PLACE FELT ON BRISTOL BOARD FACE (#**5**).

5. STITCH "BRIDGE OF BEAK" TO FELT BETWEEN EYES. CURVE IT TO FIT.

6. STITCH BEAK TO FACE FROM **X** TO **Y**.

7. NOW STITCH AROUND EYE.

8. REPEAT STEPS **6** AND **7** ON OTHER EYE.

9. STITCH BILL TOGETHER. STUFF.

10. TO KEEP STUFFING IN BILL, TACK TRAP (#**6**) ON INSIDE.

10. PAINT EYES YELLOW. DRAW IN NOSTRILS AND BEAK LINES. PUNCH HOLES FOR STRING. ATTACH STRING. GO FOR A STROLL BENDING YOUR KNEES BACKWARD.

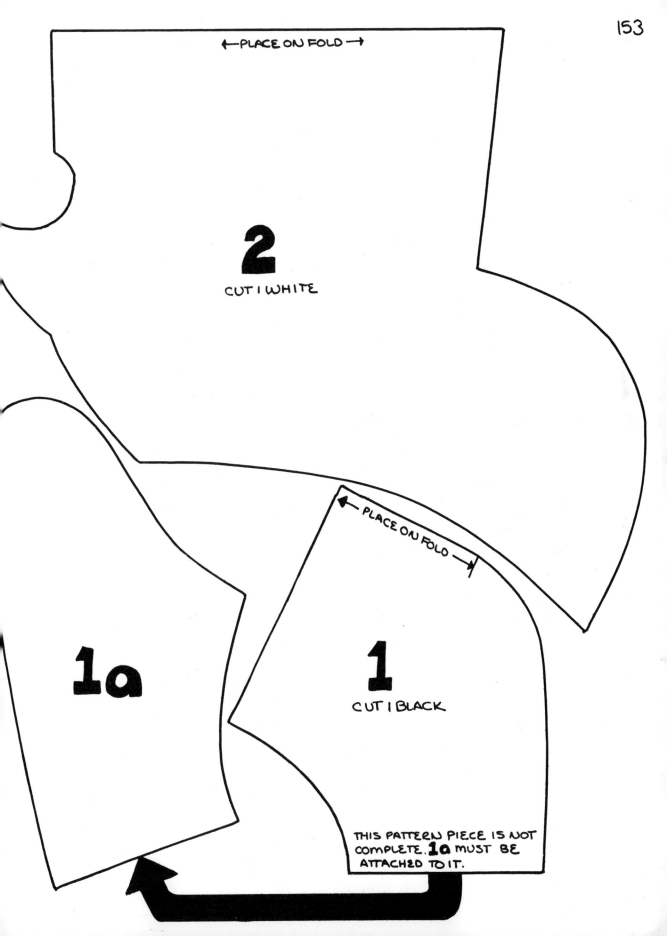

← PLACE ON FOLD →

2

CUT 1 WHITE

← PLACE ON FOLD →

1a

1

CUT 1 BLACK

THIS PATTERN PIECE IS NOT COMPLETE. **1a** MUST BE ATTACHED TO IT.

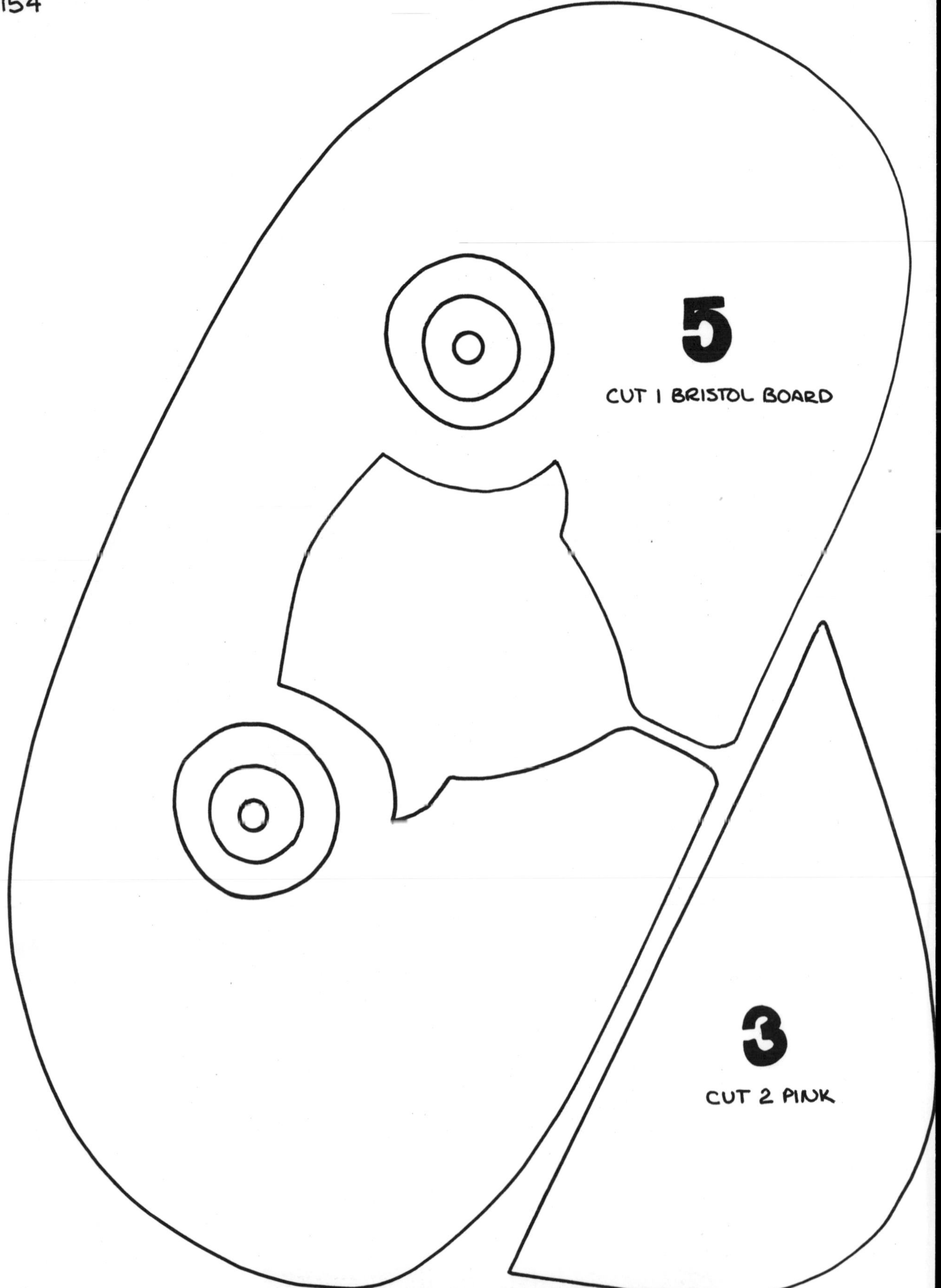

154

5

CUT 1 BRISTOL BOARD

3

CUT 2 PINK

4

CUT 1 PINK

6

CUT 1 WHITE

GOOSE MASK

YOU WILL NEED:
4"x10" BRISTOL BOARD
8"x11" PINK FELT
STRING

1. STITCH NOSTRILS TO UPPER BILL (#**2**).

2. STITCH DART IN LOWER HALF OF BILL (#**1**).

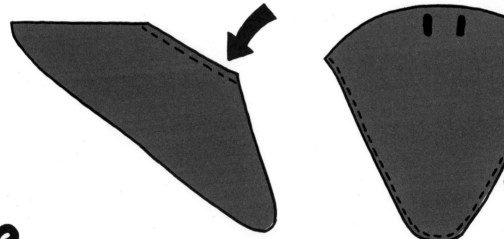

3. STITCH LOWER HALF TO UPPER HALF OF BILL.

4. CUT OUT EYE HOLES IN #**3**. DRAW WHATEVER YOU WISH ON #**3** TO TURN IT INTO AN EMPEROR GOOSE.

5. STITCH THE BILL TO THE FACE.

6. PUNCH HOLES FOR STRING. ATTACH STRING.

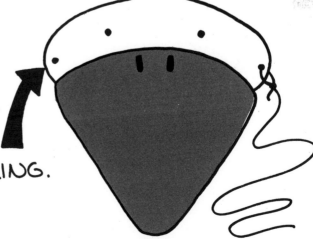

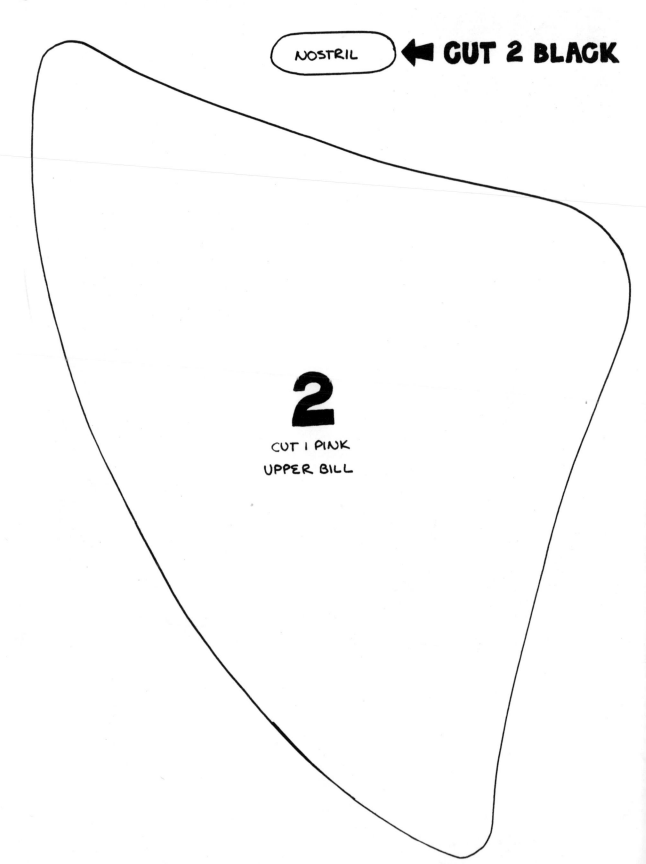

NOSTRIL ← CUT 2 BLACK

2

CUT 1 PINK

UPPER BILL

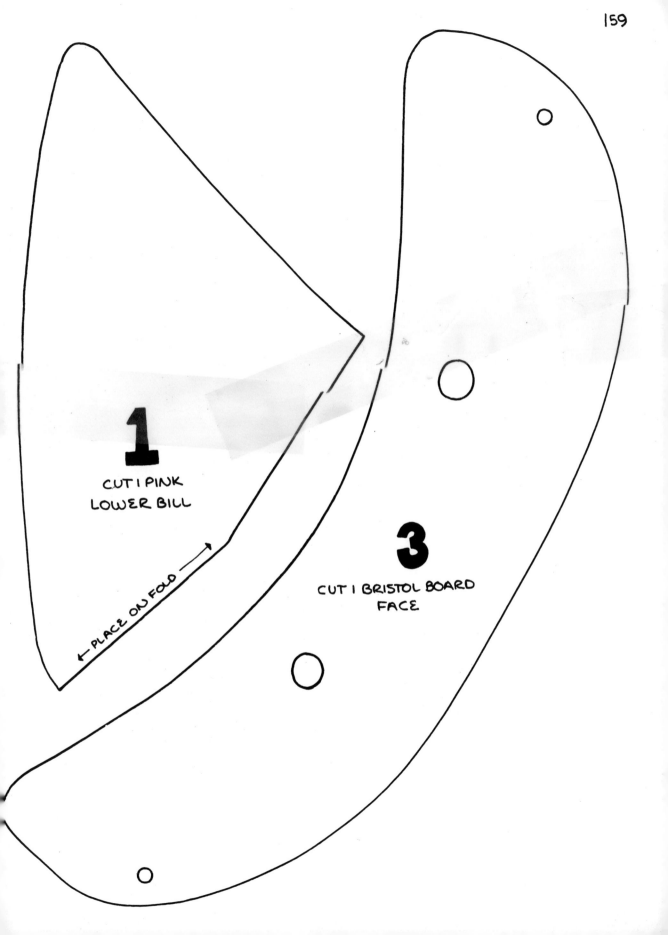

1

CUT 1 PINK
LOWER BILL

← PLACE ON FOLD →

3

CUT 1 BRISTOL BOARD
FACE

ACKNOWLEDGEMENTS

PRINTED AND BOUND BY
GRÁFICA EDITORA PRIMOR
RIO DE JANEIRO - BRAZIL

MARK SEXTON
AMY KEELER
HI·DA·WAY GREENHOUSE
COMMONWEALTH FELT CO.